Praise for
Extracting Wisdom

"Martha does an amazing job of articulating the rigors of transitioning from residency through private practice."

–Adam Flack, DDS, MD, Oral and Maxillofacial Surgeon

"This is more than a framework for an efficient and safe office; this is a guide to being fulfilled, happy, respected in the community, by patients, by colleagues, by their own office staff who will live in a culture designed to engineer the compassion, respect and satisfaction that leads to success and happiness."

–Paul J. Walters, DDS, Oral and Maxillofacial Surgeon

"What an incredible masterpiece! *Extracting Wisdom* is packed with wise and valuable information. It is the playbook for success. This book depicts a gentle yet powerful message for everyone."

–Patti Doty, RN, Oral and Maxillofacial Surgical Assistant

Answering The Call To Build High-Impact
Oral And Maxillofacial Surgery Practices
From Residency Through Retirement

EXTRACTING
WISDOM

Martha Dunlevy Peters

INDIE BOOKS
INTERNATIONAL

ISBN 13: 978-1-952233-68-5
Library of Congress Control Number: 2021914883

Book designed by SP Book Design (SPBookDesign.com)
Author headshot photographed by Cathryn Farley
INDIE BOOKS INTERNATIONAL®, INC.
2424 VISTA WAY, SUITE 316
OCEANSIDE, CA 92054
www.indiebooksintl.com

Table of Contents

Foreword

BUILDING A HIGH-IMPACT oral and maxillofacial surgery (OMS) practice from residency through retirement is dependent upon making wise decisions and adopting key processes. Identifying a practice vision, establishing a business plan, building a dynamic team, providing leadership, and finding passion in your work, all play critical roles in determining your success. The culture you adopt influences this success. The positive impact you have on your patients and the relationships you build are what matter the most. Remember, we all start somewhere and eventually we all cross the finish line. It is the beginning of your career that connects you to the end, and everything in between is your story. We rise together because no task is accomplished alone but through the collaboration of minds seeking the same outcome—exceptional patient care. May we all answer the call to contribute to a culture of excellence in OMS.

Dedication

THIS BOOK IS dedicated to P. J. Walters, DDS. Many years ago, you gave me your wings when mine were broken. You taught me to see the mountaintop from a different view by showing me that a different approach can influence the destination. It was your continual voice of encouragement and your commitment to provide compassionate care that empowered me, as a patient, to rise above surgical limitations and accept outcomes. Together, we redefined success. Sometimes the most beautiful stories come from difficult procedures. Even after thirty plus years, our special bond remains untouched. Today, you are still standing by my side as a friend and mentor, coaching and encouraging me to contribute continually to a culture of excellence in OMS. Thank you for your guidance and friendship. I am forever grateful for everything that you have done for me. Your presence in my life continues to lead me to better places. Our surgical history is a connection to your OMS past; and this book, my friend, honors that legacy.

Family Is Everything

To MY FAMILY: Eric, Sean, Connor, Teagan, Quinn, and Kathleen, the long hours to write this book have taken precious time away from each of you. Thank you for supporting me throughout this publishing process. You are my greatest source of encouragement and my greatest accomplishment. I love you all.

To my Dad: Thank you for instilling a passion for writing in me at a very early age. You showed me the beautiful connection between word usage and evoking feelings to tell a story. Your wisdom has served as a valuable guidepost as I danced along the path of life.

To my Mom: Thank you for your continued love and support. You taught me the importance of relying on faith to get through difficult situations.

Chapter 1

We All Start Somewhere

IF WALLS COULD talk, they would say a lot. Memories of 4400 Broadway, Suite 400, remain etched in my mind. This oral and maxillofacial surgery (OMS) practice was an industry leader, high-volume, fast-paced, and at times uncensored. The scope of this practice was dentoalveolar surgery, dental implants, pathology, maxillofacial trauma, orthognathic surgery, temporomandibular joint (TMJ) procedures and facial cosmetic surgery (FCS). This practice showcased unparalleled surgical skills and knowledge, which also supported the continual training of oral surgery residents who walked through the doors.

I started my surgical assistant career here, surrounded by many OMS residents who rotated through this multi-surgeon private practice setting. Working with these residents was a learning opportunity for me, just as much as it was for them. Together, we faced the day-to-day challenges of putting in long hours, assisting with back-to-back cases, and keeping up with the fast-paced tempo that this busy practice offered. We persevered through difficult procedures, adapted to office stresses, and always had each other's backs. We knew how to navigate through rough waters by standing together as a unified surgical team.

Starting early-morning cases together and assisting with after-hour emergency procedures just went with the territory. Schedules changed without warning and with that uncertainty came the critical need for effective time management and efficiency. We learned quickly how to master both. Everyone working in this specialty knows that facial fractures and incision and drainage procedures rarely happen at convenient times. The connection between flexibility and accomplishing what needed to get done became obvious. These efforts were clearly visible in our ability to effectively deliver quality patient care, especially during times of chaos. We soon realized that adaptability and accountability were important soft skills to adopt. It was here where we also learned to value relationships and appreciate kindness. At the end of the day, it was not necessarily what we did, but how well we did it, that had the most impact—on everyone.

I learned many valuable hands-on skills sitting with residents in a tiny room, down the hall from our office. It is here where I helped with model trimming and watched attentively as they fabricated surgical splints, articulated models, and traced cephalometric films. Ironically, however, the most important skill I learned here was listening. The grinding of the model trimmer and the sputtering sound of the slurry water hitting the abrasive band could not drown out important conversations. Over several years, I heard many voices—tired, stressed, happy, and excited—simply because I listened. In this small, dimly lit, dusty lab, life stories were shared: engagements, weddings, births, accomplishments, struggles and disappointments. These candid conversations captured the lives of many of my OMS residency friends. Their stories were important to me because they were important to them. I often smile, thinking of the white gypsum powder trail that followed these residents down the hall. It was a visible sign of long hours in the lab spent preparing for upcoming orthognathic cases. However, it was also a sign that they were tucked away from the stressful and demanding pressures of being an OMS resident.

Behind closed doors, I listened to their hopes and fears, but it was during surgeries—gowned, gloved, and masked—that I saw their surgical talents and confidence evolve. These opportunities also helped me develop my own surgical assisting skills. Together, we approached each case with deliberation by familiarizing ourselves with pertinent patient information, confirming the scheduled procedure, and discussing any concerns. These residents taught me more than just hands-on surgical skills, but also the importance of utilizing critical thinking, which supported prudent decisions and positive patient outcomes. When cases were finished, debriefing periods provided opportunities for all of us to reflect and evaluate our skills. We worked together as a team, building relationships through trust and honesty. We were each accountable for our actions and every uncertainty was viewed as a learning opportunity. These behaviors supported a culture of excellence. The lessons I learned from these residents years ago, still remain with me today. It is those lessons that have helped me build a credible platform, showing the importance of standing by your surgeon and connecting with your team. Through these shared moments, we developed mutual respect, deep connections, and lifelong friendships.

Needless to say, some of my most memorable career moments were spent standing alongside these residents. It was an honor to be a small part of their journeys forward. This opportunity gave me a front row seat to watch their surgical and interpersonal skills blossom as they grew into fine oral surgeons. By no means was this an easy task for them to achieve; but through hard work, commitment, and perseverance, each one eventually headed out the gate, to begin their OMS career. We all start somewhere.

Chapter 2

It's Your Business, Choose Wisely

L IFE AFTER RESIDENCY is a new chapter with many career paths. If your passion is in a private practice setting, then explore partnerships, associateships, or solo ventures. If teaching is your forte, then consider a position in the academic sector. A military career may be an option for those who are called to serve their country. Corporate opportunities may appeal to those who don't want to handle the business aspect of running a private practice directly. Make sure your employment decision meets your needs and is a good match for your talents and interests. Approaching decisions prudently and intelligently is a critical step. The decisions you make today will affect the rest of your career profoundly. Regardless of your career path or the scope of your practice, offering high-impact services should always be your main concern. High-impact OMS models exceptional patient care and supports a continual culture of excellence. Adopting this mindset will influence your career positively, no matter where you choose to practice.

Building a high-impact practice is not random like the lottery. Success takes time and it requires constant attention. It follows hard work, dedication, and meeting patient needs. It is a continual process of trial and error deliberated through reflection and corrected by remediation. Success starts by adopting a practice culture. It is this culture that influences decisions, values, and attitudes, which all coherently support the practice vision. This vision clearly defines goals, reflects leadership and management skills, supports high training standards, and models exceptional patient care. Remember, this vision is a guide, a constant reminder of core practice values, which are the reasons why you are in business. It needs to be constantly embraced and re-visited, to keep you heading in the right direction.

This vision will lead you to develop a strategic business plan, which is a tool to guide and measure your success. A business plan is the roadmap of a practice. It connects you today, with where you want to be tomorrow, by showing you how to get there. Remember, as situations evolve and change, so will your business plan. Planning and preparing for the unexpected is critical. It's an imperative skill to manage challenges and navigate detours as they arise. Keen business skills are needed daily, to support effective practice management. It's important to have good systems in place, to be able to measure progress and see results. Successful practices will set realistic goals and measure their performances against them. Frequent corrections should be expected and executed, in order to stay on course. Nothing is on auto-pilot status, ever.

The surgeon's participation in the business aspect of the practice is imperative and requires continual involvement and feedback. For many surgeons, this presents a daunting task because the necessary business skills are sometimes out of their scope of expertise. Unfortunately, many dental programs lack a strong business curriculum. The technical-surgical skills are emphasized and mastered but the business skills are often deficient or missing. A practice cannot be sustained on the surgeon's clinical skills alone. Success is dependent upon combining many skills—business, surgical, and interpersonal.

Never hesitate to reach out for business management support. There is no shame in seeking expert advice to help run your business. Seek out an accountant who understands your business model and who can focus on your specific practice needs. Also, consider connecting with a practice management consulting firm who specialize in OMS practices. They are great resources to help identify areas that need improvement. It is far better to recognize and resolve smaller problems than to ignore matters and be faced with bigger issues down the road. Problems typically don't solve themselves on their own; instead, they fester. The price tag on overlooked problems, whether with practice management or practice development, can quickly translate into significantly declining financial performance. Partnering with OMS practice management firms to assist in practice evaluations, transitions, or even long-term relationships, makes for smart business decisions.

We each have unique needs, but some of us are better at acknowledging them. So, make sure you understand the skills you have and reach out for the skills you need. You will never regret this decision. Seeking expert business management advice can prevent financial devastation in the long run. Remember, running a business in the dark is the best way to guarantee running a practice into the red.

Also, consider finding a role model. There are surgeons who would be honored to be mentors: find and connect with them. When they share their wisdom, you gain valuable knowledge. The value in their experience is priceless. Supporting a culture of excellence takes everyone's contributions and help: the young, the seasoned, and the retired. We should all want everyone to succeed because together, we are stronger and better.

Building a high-impact team requires constant attention. The first step in developing staff members is to make sure that they understand the practice culture and are aligned with your vision. The ideal team models compassion, shows integrity, and is committed to delivering exceptional patient care. Put the best players on your team and expect excellence. A high-impact team is well trained to handle any situation. Your greatest asset and investment stand by your side. Never forget this. Always provide leadership for your team by being a positive role model. Inspired teams are effective teams. Set expectations, communicate effectively, encourage continual education, teach and engage, and provide constant feedback. Strong leadership encourages staff development and supports a culture of excellence.

Finding passion along this journey is also critical to success. Successful people find contentment even when facing adversity. They choose to find the joy in the journey, even when the journey is difficult, because they embrace their vision and feel a purpose that intimately connects them to their commitment to succeed. Purpose is not what we chase: it is what we feel. Successful surgeons understand that the road to success is never easy, but they realize that all roads lead somewhere if they keep moving forward. Staying focused and on course is the most important direction.

It takes vision to build a solid business plan; it takes a leader to build a dynamic team; and it takes passion to bring it all together. However, it is the practice culture that ultimately determines this success. Building a high-impact practice comes through wise decision making and aligning yourself with processes that are vital to success: identifying a practice vision, establishing a business plan, building a dynamic team, providing leadership, and finding passion in your work. Make a commitment to connect and to do more by going above and beyond; accept nothing less. That's how you start building a high-impact practice. It's your business, so choose wisely.

Chapter 3

A Credible View

MY PERCEPTION OF a high-impact practice is unique.
It first comes from my own experiences as an oral
surgery patient. These memories are difficult to revisit, but
important to share because they give credibility to the view—
and so my story begins.

My journey as a patient started when I was thirteen years
old. I tripped and collided during Physical Education class,
flipping over a tennis court net and hitting the concrete,
chin first. It was a hard blow. I vividly remember the pain so
intense and crippling. That moment of impact changed my
life forever. Severe temporal headaches, bilateral TMJ pain,
limited range of motion, and occlusal changes soon followed.
Over the next several years, splints, braces and surgical inter-
ventions, silastic implants, orthognathic surgeries, dermal
grafts, costochondral grafts, and ostectomies became routine, repeat procedures for me. Ironically, these procedures

and experiences would prepare me for a future career as an OMS surgical assistant. Proof that we can be humbly brought to our knees and eventually rise above any storm. Sometimes struggles lead us down paths that we may have never had the opportunity to explore. It is these unplanned and, at times, difficult steps, that can eventually take us to better places.

As I recall my surgical history, my heart fills with gratitude. I am thankful for the support and compassion of many OMS teams who stood by my side, throughout difficult procedures. The memories are still fresh in my mind—the surgical gurneys, the gowns, the hats, the IV's, and repeatedly signing consents. Heading off to surgery was scary. Many times, I was alone, hundreds of miles away from home with no family by my side. Even after so many trips to the operating room, the procedures did not get easier; instead, they got harder. Surgeries were long and recoveries were difficult. The fear of waking up from repeat procedures with permanent facial droop, paralysis, or numbness were always valid concerns, for all of us. I recall the beeps, the alarms, and the reassuring voices. The pain so crushing as I would attempt to lift my head off the pillows. The Foley catheters and nasogastric tubes were always bothersome and my throat was very often irritated from long intubations. The encouragement to cough and to deep breathe were difficult tasks, especially when my head was throbbing and my jaws wired shut, after most surgeries.

I remember many post-op wheelchair rides to the OMS clinic from my hospital room. The elevator rides were always unpleasant. I also recall one instance, when the orderly hit every speed bump and every floor seemed to be a designated stop. The glances turned into long stares and I heard chatter about my appearance from complete strangers who knew nothing about my surgical struggles. I recall cradling my face as every turn down a hallway seemed like an endless roller-coaster. I was lightheaded and nauseous. Everything around me seemed like a slow-motion action movie, probably because I felt so overwhelmed.

On many occasions, when I arrived at the OMS clinic, tears would be flowing down my swollen cheeks. I remember the times when the residents carefully removed my head wrap, unrolling what seemed like layers of protection, to unveil the first post-op view. It was never what I expected. I was never prepared for the swelling and distortion. Never. Looking into the mirror was difficult. I remember time after time glancing at myself and holding back tears. There is something frightening when you don't recognize yourself in the mirror. My jaws were either wired or rubber-banded shut with heavy elastics and my lips and cheeks were swollen and shiny. Jackson-Pratt drains sometimes dangled from the incisions on both sides of my neck. It was difficult to talk after most of my surgeries. Many times, I was weak and barely able to stand without assistance. I recall pulling myself up to a standing position, for the first post-op x-rays. Each time, I prayed that the hardware looked good. Attention was frequently directed at adjusting my occlusion, if needed. These adjustments, although small, felt like huge movements and tears would frequently fill my eyes and I would grip the arms of the dental chair, especially during zygomatic wire adjustments and eventually during their removal.

The road to recovery was difficult at best. Recuperating from repeat surgeries wasn't easy because these procedures didn't follow typical post-operative expectations. Increased pain, swelling, and numbness were always expected. Limited range of motion and scar tissue formation were frequent challenges, too. Physical therapy sessions were grueling but necessary and critical to my recoveries. Conversations centered around failed implants, condylar head changes, avascular necrosis, and eventually chasing condylar hyperplasia. I had frequent discussions about setting realistic expectations to anticipate and accept possible outcomes. The increased risk with repeat procedures for permanent numbness, compromised healing, and relapse were always thoroughly explained. My opinion mattered and how I was feeling inside was never dismissed. I was always involved in making the final decision but I also relied on the expertise and guidance of skilled surgeons to help me make smart decisions.

I can't tell you how many times I wanted to give up, to be done; but dynamic OMS teams surrounded me and stood by my side, to make sure I didn't quit. They offered words of encouragement, as I would depart to the operating room one more time. The OMS surgical assistants would leave cheerful notes in my hospital room so that when I woke up from surgery, I would have something to read during my hospital stay. Everybody needs encouraging words to get them through tough times. These high-impact OMS teams were my lifeline, filling

canyons in my heart when recoveries turned into frequent disappointments. They reassured me, after many surgeries, that
the swelling would subside, and each day would get better and
better. They were right. My physical therapist, Jennifer Walters,
always pushed me to stretch one more millimeter, to reach
my post-operative inter-incisal opening (IIO) goals. She was
the voice of encouragement amongst the discouragement. I
understood that achieving this range of motion early, played a
critical role in supporting my recoveries, which was beneficial
in maintaining long-term mobility.

I was frequently asked to pucker up, smile and wink
after surgeries. These animations helped evaluate my post-
operative facial nerve status. My goofy facial expressions
were sometimes asymmetric but luckily only temporarily.
Performing these gestures made me smile. I was fortunate
to walk away with only left-sided paresthesia affecting half
of my chin and lower lip. A broken Lindemann bur made
its permanent home, hanging out on my inferior alveolar
nerve, after my last surgery in 1996. I do understand numbness, profoundly. Several years ago, the OMS surgeon who I
was working for explained to a third molar patient the dif-
ference between sensory and motor nerve injury. He lined up
his three surgical assistants in the room, including me, and
asked the patient to guess which one was numb. The patient
did not pick me. This was a great lesson to show that sensory
nerve injuries do not affect appearance or motor function.

When setbacks occurred, these high-impact teams knew to
say the right words at the right time, to comfort my fragile

heart. Timing was everything. Cracking jokes after looking at my post-operative x-rays and commenting that my jaws had more screws than a pick-up truck always brought a smile to my face. Laughing together, supported my healing process. Releasing intermaxillary fixation (IMF), adjusting and removing zygomatic wires, suture removals, Z-plasties, Risdon scar revisions, soft tissue grafts, and hardware removal in the office were not fun procedures, but I never faced these alone. On many occasions a hand would reach out to hold mine. Now, as a surgical assistant, my hand is the first to reach out and the last to let go. Numerous post-operative phone calls to check on my progress meant the world to me. Today, roles are reversed and it's me making patients smile and placing phone calls, to check on them.

My many trips to the operating room are not easily forgotten. These surgical procedures at times seemed scary, but high-impact OMS teams stood by my side and comforted me. They recognized the need to support me through tough procedures. When I wrestled with difficult recoveries that were longer than I had hoped for, I got restless. When I wanted things to happen before they unfolded, I felt anxious. It's the moments when I was connected to supportive OMS teams that supported my progress. I made it through these challenging times because of the high-impact teams standing by my side.

What we do as a surgical team and how well we do it, will affect patient outcomes—this I know. A warm smile, a gentle touch, attentive listening, a hand to hold, and words of encouragement all positively affect patients. I understand firsthand the importance of providing quality care above and beyond surgical procedures and the significant role that plays in supporting positive patient outcomes, especially mine. I modeled my career around this concept because it made a significant impact on my own recoveries. Never minimize a patient's need for compassion, ever. The fear a procedure inflicts on a patient is not nearly as significant as our response to their fear. I never share my surgical journey in great detail with patients, because the value comes not in hearing my story but rather in my ability to show compassion and empathy; that connection is unique and significant.

My personal experiences as a patient influenced my decision to become a surgical assistant and fueled my passion to help build high-impact OMS practices. I understand and appreciate the services you provide, and I know these services must be exceptional. It didn't take long for me to realize that I wanted to be a part of providing this care. Without any doubt, I knew what I wanted to do with my life, who I wanted to help, and how I wanted to make people feel. Choosing a career as an OMS surgical assistant fulfilled my purpose. The surgical journey that took me to the edge and back with challenges and setbacks became the foundation to build and shape my career. My roots were established from the patient side of the chair and these raw, real, and credible experiences taught me more skills than any college textbook. Sometimes our struggles in life take us down paths we may never have had the opportunity to explore. The career path I chose is the path I have always embraced. I've never looked back nor had any regrets. No matter where my career as a surgical assistant takes me, my view will always be first from the patient's perspective and that's a credible view.

Chapter 4

Snapshots Of Reality

MY VIEW FROM the surgical assistant side of the chair has seen the ups and downs and the triumphs and struggles of OMS practices. I have also visited with surgeons who were willing to sit down with me and discuss their practice strengths and weaknesses. As Yogi Berra once said, "You learn a lot by watching," but you also learn from listening.

I have stood next to OMS surgeons as they exited residency and ventured off into private practice. Heading out of the gate, these surgeons were confident and poised. Tremendous financial risk surrounded them, but they were humble and savvy in approaching their business undertakings. They first recognized the critical need to adopt an office culture. It was this high-performance culture that cradled and influenced every decision. Business operations and practice management processes were established and communication was effective. Long-term practice goals were identified, frequently reviewed, and updated as needed. Conflict resolution and succession planning were clearly recognized, defined, and implemented. Value was placed on building a dynamic team by employing quality staff members, who were capable of delivering exceptional patient care. Behaviors that influenced positive patient outcomes were recognized and this success was frequently celebrated. These surgeons remained involved, but not consumed, with human resource processes and decisions because they had hired business managers who were competent to assist them in managing their teams. Background checks were run on every candidate to identify potential hiring risks and random drug screenings were performed several times a year. Employee salaries were presented with contracts and all discussions remained confidential. Staff evaluations were performed at ninety days, six months, and one year, unless discussions were needed sooner. These performance reviews were implemented to measure personal growth, evaluate job performance, and recognize employee contributions to the practice. Yearly raises were determined based on meeting these criteria. These surgeons realized that stagnant salaries for dedicated team members would not support a continual culture of excellence.

The staff onboarding process was viewed as a critical opportunity to roll out expectations and define roles. Each employee was given a copy of the practice employee handbook and procedural manuals to review. Occupational Safety and Health Administration (OSHA), bloodborne pathogen, and Health Insurance Portability and Accountability Act (HIPAA) training took place before employees had any patient contact. All training was documented by both the practice manager and the clinical team coordinator. Safety and compliancy training were viewed as critical practice management measures. All surgical staff members were required to pass the Dental Anesthesia Assistant National Certification Examination (DAANCE), or a state-approved sedation monitoring course, every five years. Maintaining healthcare cardiopulmonary resuscitation (CPR) certification, completing nitrous oxide monitoring courses, as well as participating in quarterly office-based anesthesia sedation and emergency training were also expected. All expectations were explained clearly in the employee manual. These surgeons supported their team by providing continual hands-on training and educational opportunities.

Communication was effective and the work environment supported a culture where staff could ask questions and feel comfortable doing so. Holding staff meetings to keep everyone informed of office updates was viewed as a critical step to support effective practice management. Bringing the team together to voice concerns, share thoughts, and proactively find solutions to problems supported the continual growth and development of the entire practice. Everyone was given the opportunity to speak and to be heard. Respect for each other was not only expected, it was required.

Outside of the office, team-building activities and social gatherings with staff and their families provided a great opportunity to continue to nurture and develop relationships. Stepping away from the office took people away from their day-to-day work routines and brought them together on a different level. Success was always celebrated with the whole team by recognizing achievements and contributions. These celebrations encouraged everyone to become better team players.

When detours and challenges surfaced, they were handled in a timely and professional manner. These surgeons recognized that no office was immune from problems and they were prepared to handle them. They also realized that leading their team through difficulties was critical to the success of the practice. Contributions to build a high-impact practice evolved from everyone's efforts, even when faced with adversity.

A commitment to excellence continued to be the nucleus of their practices and all team members embraced that concept. These surgeons knew where they wanted to take their teams and they constantly invested in this endeavor. Their main focus was first placed on developing staff members. These surgeons saw the connection between having a well-trained team and the ability to deliver high-quality, efficient services. Even though their offices were not the biggest or the most up to date, they had dedicated and talented teams surrounding them. They knew what mattered the most and they built high-impact practices from that solid foundation. The mindset that exceptional patient care would always prevail, regardless of practice updates, was continually supported. However, these surgeons recognized that if crucial business processes were successfully executed and revenue targets achieved, then eventually the latest technology and office updates could be integrated into their practices. These surgeons valued state-of-the-art equipment and updated facilities, but they also employed good judgement by determining when their practices would invest in these upgrades. Financial stability and steady growth determined this timeline. They relied on their accountants' shrewd business skills to provide guidance on when to make these important investments. These surgeons periodically reached out to consulting firms which specialized in OMS practices for support and advice. Through these ongoing relationships, the health of their practices was strategically monitored by evaluating short-term and long-term goals, which were critical markers used to measure their success.

These surgeons adopted the right attitudes heading out of the gate, which set the stage for a great performance. They realized that reinforcing these behaviors would support a continual culture of excellence within their practices. Wise decisions affected their outcomes. These surgeons understood that their long-term success was supported by recognizing this fundamental concept. Continuing to lead their teams with passion and a commitment to excellence, these surgeons never lost sight of their aspirations and they never looked back. Many are still at the helm of these successful practices, which started out humbly and quickly grew into high-impact offices. Their footprints tell a compelling story of how they have led their teams, but more importantly, where they have taken their practices. Today, as part of their succession plans, mapped out years ago, many are preparing to hand over the reins to a younger generation of surgeons who are eager to start their OMS careers. Their greatest contributions to the OMS specialty will be their legacies, each embedded in a vision that supports a culture of excellence.

I have also watched other OMS surgeons build state-of-the-art facilities, taking on enormous financial hardships and risk. Their failure to establish a practice culture and implement a solid business plan immediately set them up for a turbulent ride as they headed out of the gate. Attitudes and values were never defined. Processes that needed to be recognized were never given much thought or attention. Office manuals and employee handbooks were rarely discussed or reviewed. Overlooking these important communication tools resulted in continual uncertainty within these practices. Problems were overlooked because no leadership was set in place to manage issues as they surfaced. Chaos and confusion became daily routines and problems continued to spiral out of control.

Leadership skills were missing, communication was deficient, and there was very little value placed on staff members. The work environment was futile—like planting grass seed during a hurricane. Roles and expectations were not established, which resulted in tasks not getting done because nobody understood their responsibilities. Failing to see the value in aligning with high-quality staff members proved disastrous. Putting the wrong players on their teams, just because they were affordable, set their practices up for failure. This was a costly mistake. The onboarding process for employee training consisted of showing up on the first day and guessing your way through processes and procedures.

The value in employee recruitment, training, and retention was not visible. Good employees did not tolerate these behaviors and they quickly made their departures.

The pressure to generate revenue quickly, in order to support their state-of-art facilities, continued to be an overwhelming task. This financial burden became a distraction and providing exceptional patient care became out of focus. The extreme overhead created significant financial stress—crippling stress, even before these practices opened their doors.

Poorly defined business models also continued to add insult to injury. There was no clear path established to roll out practice development plans or processes, which were critical steps needed to build successful offices. Investing in marketing and treatment plan coordinators before processes were established and understood by everyone proved disastrous for these offices. These surgeons learned the hard way that bringing patients through their doors too quickly, without being prepared to handle them efficiently, became the perfect set-up for failure. Patients before preparation is like putting the cart ahead of the horse.

Nothing is more damaging than sending a message to patients and to the referring community that you don't have your act together. This scenario was visible in long patient waits in the waiting room and in procedure rooms. Productivity and performance fell short for these offices. Financial problems followed them, which contributed to a constant environment of stress and chaos. These surgeons struggled to stay afloat and never became high-impact practices, because no culture was visible and essential key processes were not recognized, supported, or carried out. Proof that order does affect outcome.

I have also seen the devastating effects of sloppy finances, driven by not having a checks and balances system set in place, to see the flow of money coming in and going out. Business operations were allowed to slide continually and quickly headed into the wrong direction. Over time, book-keeping records no longer passed the litmus test and no attempts were made to identify and correct problems. The collection process was delinquent as cycled billing statements were not routinely sent out, insurance claims were not filed in a timely manner, and incorrect codes were used on exit tickets, which resulted in a flurry of denied claims that couldn't be promptly or easily rectified. The office's financial health was like a see-saw—up and down and never stable; year after year, the mess got deeper and deeper. Ultimately, financial reserves no longer existed because the pot that once held the gold had become depleted.

These surgeons saw how losing their grip on critical targets, those that measured the direction of key business operations, eventually resulted in devastating monetary consequences that rocked their practices. The repercussions were far-reaching in these offices. Technology was rarely updated because there was no money to invest in upgrades, so computer software systems were constantly bogged down and inefficient. Continuing education opportunities for staff members sank because it was difficult to invest in training when funds were just not available. Employee raises were rarely given because it was difficult at times to even make payroll. Retaining quality staff members was challenging as merit could not be recognized through fair and earned compensation measures. These practices had revolving doors for employee retention and the quality of care was affected by the frequent turnover of talented staff. The culture inside these practices were always doom and gloom. Morale was low and stress was high. Nobody was happy.

So, how did these situations evolve and what created these financial storms of chaos? The answers undoubtedly point to a lack of leadership and exercising poor business skills—nothing more, nothing less. Adopting this mindset spread turmoil into every aspect of these practices. It's an impossible task to try and create success when leadership is inadequate or non-existent and when strong business skills are not employed. These surgeons had outstanding surgical skills, but they failed to reach out for help with the business aspect of running their offices. These practices, as they aged, were not marketable to sell, nor were they appealing to prospective OMS surgeons, simply because a trail of financial dysfunction had carried these practices into unimaginable and crippling debt.

I have listened to surgeons share how they integrated facial cosmetic surgery (FCS) into their practices. Some built surgery centers accredited by the Accreditation Association for Ambulatory Health Care (AAAHC) and invested in high-profile consulting firms to market their practices. However, for many, their exemplary FCS training fellowships and talent alone were not enough, to keep them afloat in the competitive facial cosmetic surgery arena. Many saw their hopes and dreams never fully take off. Blazing a trail to showcase blending traditional OMS services with FCS was not an easy undertaking. Looking back, some of the most successful facial cosmetic surgery practices that I saw launch and succeed were those that made the decision to practice FCS exclusively and not combine both. These surgeons' success was also attributed to recognizing and implementing processes that supported exceptional patient care. Their success was influenced not only by exceptional surgical skills but also because their mindsets were tethered to high standards, which were steadfast in supporting a culture of excellence.

I have felt the effects of partner dissolutions in practices. When this separation occurs, the resulting pain, turmoil, and disruption often divide the OMS team. Staff members are faced with choosing which of the former partners to align with and these are not easy decisions. Rebound and recovery are difficult processes for everyone involved. The importance of aligning on practice management issues, decision making, conflict resolution, and succession planning must be recognized, communicated, and supported by all surgeons within the practice. Early discussions on these critical issues are needed to support healthy partnerships. These OMS surgeons did not share the same vision with their colleagues, which was critical to carry out a successful business relationship. It is this relationship that would have eventually carried them across the finish line together. High-impact practices are dependent upon leadership, honesty, trust, and effective communication, all of which support office harmony. Office harmony is needed to support a continual culture of excellence; when that harmony is not present, relationships suffer and, sadly, practices disband.

I have listened attentively to OMS surgeons share how they re-evaluated their business and practice management models. These surgeons were instrumental in pursuing change because they recognized that the directions in which they were leading their team no longer supported their visions. They hungered for more and were not satisfied by settling for less. Acknowledging the need to implement new or improved processes to support better patient care, as well as exploring opportunities to increase practice growth and revenue, became their catalyst for change. They understood that high-impact practices viewed reflection not as a weakness but as a strength. Their success was dependent upon recognizing the need to change their course when the direction in which they were heading no longer supported a continual culture of excellence. Simply by changing their course, these offices eventually became high-impact practices.

The surgeon who shared his humble practice beginnings with me, over a cup of coffee, will always stick in my mind. His story was both simple and engrossing. The sign on his front door read "Welcome Patients." The first year in practice was rough but it was necessary. He learned through trial and error. He started out with a shoestring staff of two team members, training and treating them well. They stood by his side every day, riding out the ups and downs of building a practice from ground zero. Finances were tight. He paid his staff before he paid himself. Thrift store deals furnished his waiting room, but it was comfortable and inviting. His equipment was gently used but it got the job done. He knew there were things he wanted, but he only bought the things he needed. There were days when he only had a few patients; on other days, he had none. Some days the phone didn't even ring. On many occasions, he came in early and stayed late to accommodate patients. He placed a small ad in the local newspaper letting the community know he was available. Eventually the practice name was also found tucked deep within the Yellow Pages. Ironically, he smiled as he recalled most patients telling him that they found his practice through word of mouth.

He believed that every patient deserved exceptional quality care and that a happy patient was the best patient. He also walked door-to-door, letting dentists know that he was available to see their patients. Some welcomed him, while others did not. He remained available, patient and kind—to everyone. Honesty and compassion were always visible in the services he provided. His practice took off because of those values. The wrinkles on his face and calloused hands were etchings of hard work and long hours providing patient care. His profound wisdom resonated when he shared the secret to his success with me. His words flowed so eloquently, no doubt because they were so intentional: "Always focus on the things that matter. The one-tooth local is just as important as the set of thirds. In the end, it's the exceptional care you give every patient that builds your practice." This mindset sustained his forty-five-year OMS career. This surgeon did not find success—he created it by answering the call to serve one patient at a time.

Finally, I have watched OMS surgeons wrestle with the difficult decision of whether to continue practicing in the private practice sector or to consider pursuing academic opportunities that seemed more fitting at that time in their careers. Many valid reasons existed to support this decision to make a career change and all of them were very personal and unique. Change is initiated within but can be quickly shut down by outside influences. One must never be influenced by the fear of failing at new endeavors. Failure only occurs when one stops believing that they can do something.

Stepping out of our comfort zones and taking chances echoes uncertainty but it also mirrors courage. It is what's inside our hearts and minds that determines our willpower to support this change. Experiences give us opportunities and until we have tried something, we cannot truly evaluate the fit. We are never prisoners of our decisions if we view them as opportunities to further our growth and development. We can always go back to where we started; but one cannot ever recapture a missed opportunity. If what you are doing today isn't what you want to do tomorrow, then change course. A career is a journey, and that journey will eventually lead you down the right path if you remember to embrace the change that supports your cause.

I have seen first-hand and through opportunities to sit down and talk with surgeons, how some have become high-impact practices and why some struggle. The differences that separate the two are profound. When you fail to adopt a practice culture, you struggle. When you cannot lead and inspire a team, you struggle. When no value is placed on staff, you struggle. When acquiring too much practice debt becomes a financial burden, you struggle. When you are too worried about patient volume, instead of quality of care, you struggle. When you lose focus on the things that matter, you struggle. When you forget to practice humility, you struggle. When you focus on surgical skills alone and overlook business and interpersonal skills, you struggle. When you cannot empower your patients, you struggle. When you allow the fear of change to hold you back from exploring opportunities, you struggle.

Nothing crushes success quicker than a lack of leadership, poor communication, deficient management skills, and poor-quality care. Performance, patient care, and productivity will fall short if critical business and practice management processes are not recognized, implemented, and maintained. High-impact practices understand that their success is dependent upon the culture they adopt. That culture is supported by aligning with key processes—identifying a practice vision, establishing a business plan, building a dynamic team, providing leadership, and finding passion in your work. When those attitudes are recognized and adopted, success is achievable.

The surgeons who I have stood by throughout my career, as well as those who have welcomed me into their practices to observe and share their stories, have all been invaluable sources of knowledge. Their willingness to teach and share provided me with up-close and transparent views. All of these opportunities have contributed to this book and bring credibility and value in defining how to support a culture of excellence.

To those who have headed out of the gate and never looked back, recognizing and implementing key processes that are critical to success—well done. To those who have encountered steep climbs or have fallen short—remember that struggles teach us all humility. Keep going forward. To those who have experienced the dissolution of partnerships—may this experience be a valuable lesson for all of us on the importance of alignment to support long-term partner relationships. To those who have found the courage to turn their practices around— may we all realize that hitting the reset button is always an option. To those who have shared their wisdom so that others may benefit from it—remember, your story can influence their story. To those who are passionate about practicing FCS, let nothing impede your passion. To those who have changed the course of their practices through reflection—your stepping back to look at your practice helps you step up. To those who have changed the direction of their career paths—embrace this new opportunity. Courage and confidence propel one forward. It is sharing these snapshots of reality that help all of us better understand and appreciate why some practices struggle and why some succeed in becoming high-impact offices.

Chapter 5

Career-Defining Moments

THROUGHOUT MY CAREER as a surgical assistant, career-defining moments have captured the true meaning of high-impact OMS. These experiences taught lessons, developed skills, told stories, empowered minds, and even touched hearts. They also conveyed emotions, demanded patience, demonstrated understanding, and offered wisdom, all of which are needed to support a continual culture of excellence. These memories reinforced the message of why we all do what we do as OMS providers and surgical supportive staff—to deliver exceptional patient care.

Within a few months of starting my career as a surgical assistant, I saw how routine interactions with patients impacted their care positively, especially when I took the time to listen attentively and show compassion. My surgical assistant skills were not yet developed, and I knew very little about instrumentation, airways, or procedures but what I did know was that the most important skills to first employ, were my interpersonal skills. No doubt my own experiences as an OMS patient influenced this connection. But what I didn't realize was how these opportunities would develop me as a surgical assistant and positively influence me as a person. These experiences left me with lasting impressions, only because they were so powerful and their messages so strong; these are the patient stories and the career-defining moments worth sharing.

I vividly remember the day that John, an older gentleman, came to our office for an intraoral lesion consultation and excision biopsy. Wearing a torn black trench coat, he appeared to be a quiet man, his demeanor very gentle and reserved. His smile radiated a softness and the sparkle in his eyes held my attention as I reviewed his health history. After performing a thorough clinical examination, my surgeon proceeded with a biopsy. I reassured John that our office would be available around the clock to answer any post-operative questions or concerns that arose. Again, his eyes sparkled, almost dancing as I told him I would call to check on him before leaving the office that evening. John quickly reached out his hand and grabbed mine as he uttered the words, "Thank you, my dear, thank you."

Several days later, he received a phone call from our office asking him to come in to discuss the pathology report, which confirmed invasive squamous cell carcinoma. I can still picture him sitting in the dental chair, his wrinkled face drawn, as the surgeon explained, in great detail, the need to schedule a hospital surgical procedure as soon as possible. This necessary surgery would not be easy. The gentleness that once surrounded John was now replaced with fear. His eyes teared up and he gripped a piece of paper as the surgeon left the room. I wheeled my chair next to John's and reached out and held his hand. He explained to me that he lived with his elderly sister, who was in her nineties, and he was worried about who would take care of her while he was in the hospital recovering. The paper he was holding had his sister's phone number scribbled down on it. At this moment, I realized that John put the needs of others before his own. His baby-blue eyes filled with tears again as he shared with me his fear of undergoing the procedure and the possibility of a disappointing outcome. I said nothing until John finished speaking, because my job was simply to listen and to be a comforting presence in the room.

It was late afternoon on a cool fall day when we took John into surgery. I remember sitting in the hospital locker room, patiently waiting for our operating room to open up. I decided to walk over to the pre-operative holding area to visit John. When I walked into the room, his eyes greeted me, once again with that familiar sparkle. He reached out both arms and squeezed my hands and quietly said, "Thank you for being here, Martha." Then he handed me a crumpled-up piece of paper with a phone number listed and asked me to call his sister after surgery, to let her know he was okay. I understood how difficult heading into surgery can be when family is not present because I had been alone for many of my procedures. I reassured him that I would stand by his side, not only during the procedure, but also throughout his recovery. Showing compassion and support is an essential part of any recovery process—this I know.

This was my first opportunity to assist with a mandibular resection procedure with external fixation. However, it was not the first time that I supported a patient emotionally, through a tough procedure. Surgery was long and tedious. I remember the resection was quite extensive. We used an endotracheal (ET) tube, filled it with acrylic material and screwed it externally to the angle of his jaw. The challenge for me was mixing the acrylic quickly, getting it pumped inside the ET tube, and bending it perfectly into a horseshoe shape, before it set up. It took me several attempts to get it done. This surgical procedure was difficult. My surgical assisting skills were challenged. Several hours later, the team exited the operating room; the prognosis was poor. For many reasons, this particular case left a lasting impression on me.

Before leaving the hospital that evening, I placed the phone call to John's sister to let her know that he was out of surgery. I also checked on John in the post-op holding area. He was resting comfortably but looking down at his swollen face brought back a flood of my own memories as I remembered being a patient in the recovery room, too. Holding his hand, I quietly whispered, "Surgery is finished. I called your sister. I will see you tomorrow. Stay strong, my friend." I stood by his bed for a few minutes, listening to the familiar beeps and sounds of the monitors as they cycled yet another time. I watched his chest rise and fall, hoping and praying that the surgery had been successful and that his post-operative period would be uneventful. On many occasions, during my own post-operative recoveries, I found myself praying for this same outcome.

The next morning, I was scheduled to assist in the operating room with another case, so I popped in to visit John on my way into surgery. The first words he mumbled to me were, "Thank you for holding my hand last night." He was struggling to eat breakfast and was overwhelmed with post-operative pain. I had experienced that same situation many times myself. I knew that what he needed most was a hand to hold and to hear a voice of reassurance. My eyes met his, with empathy, as I gently placed the syringe to his lips, squirting in the protein supplement, one cc at a time. Carefully wiping his chin and encouraging him to keep going, we eventually got the job done. A small but noticeable smile creeped toward the sides of his puffy cheeks. The moments when we do ordinary things but see remarkable results are often simply because we do things together.

John's recovery was slow and painful and he needed a lot of encouragement. Again, I knew the importance of compassionate care, first-hand. He requested that his weekly post-operative appointments be coordinated on the days I was working in the Plaza office. These weekly check-ups even though not under ideal situations, gave him a chance to seek comfort and most importantly, to feel anchored. I got the honor of shaving his face every week as the external fixation was challenging for him to shave around at home, on his own. We used to joke with each other because he would sit in the dental chair for his weekly shave and I frequently reminded him that I had no skills in performing this task; nevertheless, he was a repeat client week after week. Without a doubt, my shaving skills were not proficient but he was too kind to say anything. Truthfully, he really didn't show up to get the clean-cut look anyway; instead, he came to feel supported and left feeling connected. Connections are vital to survival, as I know from my own surgical journey.

Several months went by and John was still coming into our office for follow-up care. It was during these appointments that I got to really know and understand him. He was smart and articulate. He was scared. John was human and he cried. Occasionally he was late for his appointments because he missed the bus, but he was apologetic. He enjoyed Frank Sinatra and blueberry pie. His only vice was having smoked a pipe for fifty years, which likely contributed to his oral cancer. He was a bachelor, who devoted his time and attention to taking care of the poor and downtrodden and, later in life, his elderly sister. He was not financially wealthy, but he was rich in kindness. He was a storyteller, a dreamer, a doer, and a great dancer. John taught me to waltz in the operatory, while waiting for his appointments. He was patient. I taught him how to dance the macarena. He was a good sport.

Over the next several months, more surgical procedures were performed and his recoveries became increasingly difficult. My hand held his before heading into the operating room and my voice was the first voice, he heard in the recovery room. He always felt my presence and he knew that no matter the outcome, I would stand by his side. Other serious health challenges soon surfaced amongst the storm he was already battling. John knew his time was limited, but he nonetheless modeled courage. One evening, I received a phone call from the OMS resident who was taking calls for our office. He told me that John had contacted the after-hours answering service multiple times, requesting that he be put in touch with me. He had not seen me at his last appointment because I was recovering from my own hardware removal. After receiving this message, I contacted John at home and asked him politely what I could do for him. He grilled me with questions: "Martha, are you okay? I missed you last week, how is your jaw feeling? I'm worried about you. What can you eat? Do you like ice cream? When will you be back to work?" Again, the concern he showed for others was apparent.

A few days later, he showed up at the Plaza office, this time not for an appointment but to bring me ice cream. John, freshly shaven but visibly weak and failing, handed me a sundae and a crumpled-up piece of paper. He explained that the taxicab he had taken to get to the office had no air conditioning and the melting ice cream had dripped down the side of the cup. His thoughtfulness touched my heart but it's the words he wrote on that paper that I have never forgotten: "Thank you for holding my hand, my friend. John."

I learned a lot from John in that short year. He taught a young and inexperienced twenty-three-year-old surgical assistant that time was one of life's greatest gifts and what we do with this time and the patients we affect are what matter the most. My role was simply to show compassion. Looking back, this was my most important job. Retracting in the operating room, holding a suction tip for post-operative care, or positioning him in the x-ray machine were all technical skills that really didn't matter to John. It was the eye contact, the hand to hold, the voice of reassurance, the follow-up phone calls, the dances, that mattered the most.

I will remember John for the twinkle in his eyes, his soft disposition, and thoughtfulness; however, his acceptance of a tough diagnosis has always gripped my heart. I have thought of him frequently throughout my career. The greatest lesson he taught me was that our interpersonal skills play a critical role in patient care, no matter the outcome. We all need to take the time to listen with intention, to show compassion, to make ourselves available to meet patient needs, to live in the moment—even stopping to share ice cream with a friend. I recall the day I read his obituary in the *Kansas City Star*. John was survived by his older sister and loved by many.

I reached out to Stephanie, an orthognathic and TMJ patient in our office, who was struggling to accept outcomes after multiple open joint procedures. I understood her disappointments because I too had been in that familiar place so many times myself. I listened to her concerns and supported her through many physical therapy appointments by encouraging her to stick with the program because better days were ahead, if she gave 100 percent effort. These sessions were difficult to endure as stretching exercises were not easy for her to perform. When she believed that pushing one more millimeter was not achievable, I stood on the sidelines and coached her to keep going. I knew she could do it—and she did. I saw her life improve positively within a matter of weeks once she decided to get on board with a structured physical therapy program that supported continual range of motion exercises. Positive reinforcement and encouragement can be life-changing when we empower people to believe that they can overcome challenges—this I know. A few years later, I was honored to be a part of her wedding party and watch her walk down the aisle, pain-free and smiling. She also stood at the altar on my own wedding day. Our friendship was connected by her TMJ surgical history but most importantly by her successful recovery.

I could relate to Josh, our double-jaw orthognathic surgery patient because I understood first-hand the physical and emotional transformations that came with these procedures. I realized the challenges all too well of IMF, heavy elastics, and surgical splints. Sharing pre-operative and post-operative photographs of my own surgical journeys helped reassure Josh, and many other jaw surgery patients, that their swelling would eventually resolve and that their pain was only temporary. I also shared a brochure that I had put together on normal expectations following jaw surgery. This resource became the "go-to" for many patients' questions and answers regarding post-op care. Patients typically do better when they have questions answered and understand expectations.

My liquid diet recommendations, written specifically for the recovering jaw surgery patient like Josh, were also valuable. He even contributed some of his own favorite recipes to my collection. Patient education and supportive measures are the little things that mean a lot. Anything we can do to help support a patient's recovery process is worth doing. Before he headed off to college, Josh stopped by our office several months after his procedure to say, thank you. He gave me a hand-written letter with the sweetest message: "Thank you for sticking by my side when I needed reassurance that better days were ahead. Thank you for showing me the way." I still have this card after all those years. It's a keepsake.

I met Tara, a trauma patient, late one Friday evening in the operating room. She had been involved in a motor vehicle accident and presented with multiple facial fractures and significant lacerations to her face. I will never forget scrubbing her case. Rebuilding shattered bones and performing soft tissue repairs were not easy procedures, but the surgeons who I stood beside painstakingly accomplished this task. Every suture, screw, and bone plate were placed with one purpose—to put Tara's face back together, like a jigsaw puzzle. It's opportunities like this that showcase a surgeon's intensive OMS training, by applying their knowledge and skills to weave together a shattered face. During this surgery, I saw and appreciated the true talent that this specialty holds. It also became apparent to me that OMS was more medical than dental. Without a doubt, OMS harmoniously bridges the two fields together.

Tara's recovery was difficult. The pain, the swelling, the numbness, the stitches, and the staples were overwhelming for this nineteen-year-old. She had a lot of information to process and a tough, slow road to recovery. Learning to adapt to physical changes by accepting facial scars and disfiguration were not easy. I could see her spirit was broken. Connecting with her was one way to help restore her beauty, her confidence, and her spark. I sat with her in the hospital and later in our office during post-operative appointments, reassuring her that each day she would notice improvements, even if they were small steps. People need to feel compassion and they need to feel understood. My role as a surgical assistant was to be a voice of reassurance and support, encouraging her to accept surgical limitations and outcomes. On many occasions, I pointed out to her that real beauty comes from within and nothing on the outside changes that.

My surgical journey did not involve trauma procedures, however, Tara and I were both facial reconstruction patients. We could easily identify with each other, because we each had experienced the need to feel comforted and the need to be understood. We both sat in familiar spots—facing fear and eventually accepting outcomes that weren't always ideal. Tara made a full recovery and, after months of rehabilitation, she reclaimed her sparkle and shine. She was the perfect example that one can move mountains, if they choose to rise above difficulties. It was remarkable to watch her persevere through so many surgical challenges and accept her imperfections with grace. A year after her accident, during one of her final post-operative visits, she handed me a handmade beaded bracelet that spelled out, "Strength is real beauty." This will always be one of my greatest treasures.

It was July of 1993, my first summer working in OMS. We were slammed busy and short on staff, but I always made sure that our patients received first-class care, regardless of whether we were running behind schedule. I was discharging patients from the recovery room and bringing back the next surgery, when I was summoned to the front desk to take a post-operative phone call from a concerned patient. I sat behind the glass window and answered the call without hesitation and I took the time to listen to their concerns because I viewed every question as important.

A family member of one of our patients was sitting in the lobby, while his mother was having multiple extractions performed. While waiting, he wrote me a poem and handed it to our front desk personnel. At the end of the day, Anne, our office manager gave me that poem. She said that this gentleman told her he had been watching me through the glass panel as I interacted with patients and spoke on the phone. Sometimes we don't realize that people pay attention to our body language. Sometimes we don't think that what we say and do matters, but it does. I have kept this poem framed on my desk after all of these years, as a reminder that every interaction with a patient is an opportunity to provide exceptional care and that our compassion and commitment are noticed by others.

Given With A Smile

A flash of a beautiful soul walking by
A recognition of beauty, eternal, clear, free, true.
A smile, a warmth.
That is the nature of wonder.
I will soon
Go dancing
Along the sacred path of life,
But before I do,
I want you to know,
That I saw you
Your warmth, your realness
Your beauty.
And I say to you,
Keep on smiling, keep on brightening
The lives of those around you.
Please take this poem,
As a simple gift from a stranger
Practicing the art,
Of random kindness.
—Anonymous

In our specialty, you never know what challenging cases may walk through the door or what life stories patients may share with you. Sometimes it's the four-year-old trying your patience who teaches you understanding. Sometimes it's the ninety-five-year-old who hungers for conversation and inadvertently shares wisdom. Some of my most meaningful conversations have been with patients, complete strangers, who came into our office seeking help not only for complex procedures, but for simple ones as well. I always made myself available to patients by listening and reaching across the chair to offer comfort, regardless of what services they needed. Taking the time to understand diverse needs builds patient rapport and supports a culture of excellence. Whether offering a friendly smile, a gentle handshake, or comforting words, I did it with purpose for the patient and passion for this specialty.

The duties of a surgical assistant are much more than holding a suction tip, passing an instrument, or assisting in airway management. Our role encompasses supporting the patient through any procedure, emotionally and physically. When we connect with patients by offering more than our hands-on clinical skills, we are able to provide better patient services and that's what high-impact OMS is all about. We must all remember the reason why we are here, because what we do and how well we do it will affect patient outcomes. Routine patient interactions taught me extraordinary lessons. These lessons not only made me a better surgical assistant, but a better person, too. Looking back, it's the patients I never saw coming who changed my life. It's been an honor to be a part of so many patients' surgical journeys. Career-defining moments are the ones that you remember because they never leave your heart.

Chapter 6

Golden Opportunities

I HAVE HAD THE privilege to work with many talented surgeons who willingly shared their knowledge and time with
me through countless teaching and training opportunities. I
stood next to these surgeons bumping heads, passing instruments, monitoring patients, holding airways, retracting, and
suctioning. I also watched these surgeons manage their practices, lead their teams, train residents, interact with patients,
and continually contribute to this specialty. These were all
opportunities for me to develop my career as a surgical assistant both in hands-on and in interpersonal skills. I understood that an important component of this learning process
was my willingness to be led.

I will never forget where my career started. My first
employer, Dr. David L. Moore, hired me right out of college
to work as a surgical assistant in his multi-surgeon private-
practice OMS office, which also was an outlet that supported

the oral surgery residency training program. Dr. Moore was always a teacher and I was always willing to be his student. The value he placed on continuing education was apparent. He encouraged all of his surgical assistants to become certified OMS assistants and expected them to pass Advanced Cardiovascular Life Support (ACLS) exams every two years. He sponsored many continuing education opportunities within his practice to showcase laser-assisted uvulopalatoplasty (LAUP) procedures and dental implants. He was a true leader in the OMS field, particularly when performing orthognathic surgery, as he strived for excellence and perfection in his work by teaching residents, colleagues, and staff to appreciate this life-changing procedure. I recognized his passion and dedication to OMS immediately after joining his surgical team.

He willingly shared his expertise and talent with me. I vividly remember him showing me where to place my suction tip, pointing out the exact, the perfect spot, as he painstakingly explained the mechanics of effective suctioning. He also showed me what he thought was the best way to secure an IV line by applying the tape precisely over the valley that he would make after pinching the skin together. This technique, he so relentlessly demonstrated, always worked. He demanded excellence from his surgical team. Mistakes were used as learning opportunities, even though remediation seemed at times to occur under less-than-ideal conditions. No doubt I became a better surgical assistant because my performance was under constant scrutiny; and with that watchful eye came prompt redirection as needed. Looking back, there were moments of tears and frustrations, but experiencing those emotions early in my career created a foundation for my ongoing development. The experience made me tougher, wiser, and better. Dr. Moore set high expectations and expected nothing less. I saw the value he placed on doing things the right way because that way supported a culture of excellence. Like all of us, he was not without faults and at times did not see eye-to-eye with his colleagues and staff, but his passion and commitment for this specialty never wavered, ever.

Dr. Moore recognized the spark in my eye and the hunger for knowledge that gripped my soul as I stood by his side, procedure after procedure, day after day. Recognizing this passion, he took me to my first American Association of Oral and Maxillofacial Surgeons (AAOMS) annual meeting in 1994, in Denver, Colorado. I was twenty-two years old, right out of college, and had only been working for him for a short time. I didn't comprehend the importance that surrounded that first national meeting; but today, I do understand the value in bringing people together to educate minds and to collaborate. The canopy that unites an organization and solidifies a specialty evolves from the continual contributions that support the cause we should all strive for—creating a culture of excellence. Exposing me to these meetings immersed me with a view of the full scope of OMS knowledge: educational, clinical, research, and scientific. Lifelong friendships, networking opportunities, and practice connections were made at these yearly gatherings and I am forever grateful for the opportunity to attend.

Dr. Moore's practice offered me so many opportunities to develop my surgical assisting skills. One skill became very near and dear to my heart: orthognathic surgery. I recall sitting in on numerous orthognathic surgery pre-operative consultations—bilateral sagittal splints, Le Fort I's, double jaws. I remember taking notes as my surgeons took measurements on overjet, overbite, centric relation, occlusal cant, and IIO. The opportunity to be a part of this pre-surgical process exposed me to such technical skills as taking impressions, cephalometric tracings, photographs, wax bites, face-bow transfers, fabricating surgical splints, and, eventually, articulating models. However, it also taught me to view orthognathic surgery as much more than a surgical procedure. Rather, it is a calculated process of gathering accurate records, reviewing the findings, and bringing that information together to create a desired anatomical change, a masterpiece, surgically, in the operating room. How well I know that this change created physical and, at times, emotional transformations. There is something special about being a part of a team that changes the structure of a patient's oral architecture and seeing the effect that has on improved occlusal function, facial harmony, and self-esteem. It's an amazing process to watch evolve. It is truly an art. It was a gratifying experience for me, as a surgical assistant, to play a small role in a surgical journey that started out as an initial consultation, then progressed to a pre-operative work-up, and eventually ended in the operating room.

It was the hours spent in surgery, standing alongside surgeons and residents, that truly became incredible learning opportunities for me. These cases were long and tedious but always rewarding. Head-to-head, shoulder-to-shoulder, and hand-to-hand we all stood together as a unified OMS team performing life changing procedures. I recall the moments the first incisions were made using a Bovie unit and a Colorado needle tip. These incisions, so precise along the anterior mucosa of the mandibular ramus, stripping the mucoperiosteum and temporalis muscle tendon on both the anterior mandibular ramus lateral and the medial borders. I remember always handing off the hemostat retractor to be placed on the coronoid process, to assist the surgeon in retracting the mucoperiosteum, in a superior manner. Great attention was always taken to protect the inferior alveolar nerve with a medial dissection. When the medial osteotomy was made with the Lindemann bur, my job was to irrigate with copious irrigation. I will always remember being told during my first orthognathic case, "Irrigate on the bur. Aim for the bur. We don't want to overheat the bone."

Next, under direction from the surgeon, the resident carefully completed the sagittal cut with the Lindemann bur. I would hold the inferior border retractor on the inferior border of the mandible while the osteotomy was completed. Buccal cuts were then made using both Lindemann and side-cutting fissure burs. My job was to switch out burs at the appropriate time. It took several cases before I became familiar and proficient at knowing what burs to use and when to use them. I never let the fear of unfamiliarity get in the way of a learning opportunity. Attention was then focused on the other side and the exact steps were repeated. I then packed both surgical sites with gauze. On several occasions, after the sagittal splits were completed, I would hear Dr. Hugo Obwegeser's name mentioned. One of my surgeons had had the privilege of training under him, in Switzerland many years ago. He spoke with respect and appreciation about the father of modern orthognathic surgery. No doubt, as an orthognathic patient, I also owed gratitude to Dr. Obwegeser for his relentless contributions to create facial harmony and function.

The surgeons next focused on the maxilla, with the Bovie making an incision through the mucosa and overlying musculature and periosteum. Soon, I could see the anterior maxilla as well as the maxillary tuberosity regions. The nasal mucosa was gently separated, and great protection was focused on the floor of the nose, near the piriform rim. I gently held the Freer elevator to protect the nasal mucosa at the piriform rim apertures, while the surgeon and resident completed the Le Fort I osteotomies. My other hand again, copiously irrigated on the fissure bur, during these cuts. I passed the osteotome to be used to separate the posterior maxilla from the pterygoid plates. My surgeons always explained that they would place their fingers on the palate during separation to protect the palatal tissues from tearing. These surgeons shared so much knowledge with me by patiently teaching me the "how" so I could understand the "why." I was constantly immersed in the learning process, but this was how I learned to become a skilled assistant. I had moments of uncertainty, but I always knew that the team standing next to me would support me. They were the best teachers.

Great care was also taken to protect the nasal septum and lateral nasal wall as they were separated from the maxilla with guarded osteotomes. A guide point was made at the anterior maxilla to measure the amount of impaction needed. I always wrote down these exact measurements using a skin marker on the sterile field. I learned that precise details were critical to the success of these procedures. It takes an observant team to pay attention to these details.

The moment of truth came when the maxilla was down-fractured. I remember the surgeons alerting the anesthesia team before this step took place, so the team could control the patients' blood pressure in hopes of preventing excessive blood loss. It is here where I saw the importance of controlled hypotension and how achieving it greatly improves surgical field conditions. I also better understood and appreciated why I had donated autologous blood two weeks before my own Le Fort procedures. The reason behind these blood bank visits now made perfect sense. The down fracture, completed by digital pressure, amazed me as it always seemed smooth and done with very little force. I also remember being told to be very careful with my suction tip. Specifically, one of my surgeons used to tell me, "Stay out of this area, because the brain is pretty close." That might have been the moment that influenced my hesitation, as a patient, to undergo more upper jaw procedures. Side-cutting rongeurs and sometimes a pear-shaped bur was used to trim the maxilla, allowing posterior and anterior impaction to occur. The greater palatine arteries were always pointed out to me. It was explained in great detail that the blood supply for the Le Fort I segment was provided by the ascending palatine branch of the facial artery as well as the anterior branch of the ascending pharyngeal artery. This anatomy lesson hit home several times when brisk bleeding episodes were encountered. Experience with the bipolar cautery proved that eventually all bleeding does stop when we respond quickly, calmly, and skillfully.

Finally, it was time to place the intermediate surgical splint, to position the maxilla, and to hold it in place with twenty-four-gauge wire. This was where I saw the importance of accurate pre-operative records and planning because the new position of the maxilla reflects those measurements. The patient was placed in maxillomandibular fixation, but first making sure the condyles were properly seated in the fossa—another issue very near and dear to my heart. Autorotation of the maxilla occurred, and bone plates and screws were placed. I remember great attention was focused on the V-Y closure. Gently, I held the skin hook to advance the mucosa. It is here where I learned about mattress, interrupted, and running sutures and the role they play on facial aesthetics. These surgeons took the time to explain to me that the soft tissue changes, usually resulting from a Le Fort I, can influence how the upper lip rests. How they managed these nasolabial changes during closing would ultimately affect the final aesthetic result. Their attention to detail taught me that we need to view not just the up-close view but rather the whole picture. It's the small things that actually have an impact on and influence aesthetics.

Next, our attention focused back on the mandible. A bite block was placed and I carefully helped remove the previously placed mandibular packs. I gently held the inferior and anterior border retractor while the surgeons used osteotomes to complete the sagittal split osteotomies on both sides. Occasionally, the inferior alveolar nerve would be damaged during the osteotomy procedure. Nobody in the operating room understood and accepted this situation better than I did. Watching the nerve become freed and reapproximated intrigued me. The intermediate splint was removed, and the final surgical splint was placed with wire fixation, to support the final maxillary and mandibular position. Stab incisions were made over the proximal segments, bilaterally. These incisions were used to advance the trocar through with a sharp obturator. I held the cheek retractor until the obturator was removed. Transosseous bicortical screws were then placed on both mandibular rami. Throughout the drilling process, the surgeons explained to me the importance of positioning the mandibular angles into a passive position with proper alignment at the inferior border. Incisions were then closed after copious irrigation. I always helped the resident place the compression Jobst wrap around the patient's face, in an effort to reduce swelling and to provide gentle support. It was another procedure in the books, and it was an honor to be a part of this talented OMS team as they performed this incredible procedure. I know how life-changing this surgery is from my own personal experience as an orthognathic patient.

Emerging together from the operating room, after performing these surgeries was fulfilling for me. It is here where I learned to suction, follow, retract, pass, and anticipate needs. It is also here, under the bright lights and cascade of blue drapes, that I learned to appreciate orthognathic surgery as an art because the hands that made it happen were so skilled, the results were so amazing, and the long-term benefits were undoubtedly life-changing.

These surgeons connected with their surgical teams by directing and supporting us and by continually providing an environment of rich opportunity. It was truly an honor to stand by these surgeons. The long hours assisting them in surgery provided invaluable learning opportunities and many lasting impressions. Some memories are more meaningful than others and are worthy of sharing. I recall standing next to Dr. Bob Hiatt, holding the suction tip, during a double-jaw procedure. Brisk bleeding was encountered during the down-fracture of the maxilla. His grace and voice of reassurance brought confidence to the team. Hidden behind his sturdy frame was a gentleness. As I suctioned painstakingly, I felt his softness when he glanced at me with nodding approval. During this stressful situation, this encouragement meant everything to a novice surgical assistant. He taught me to remain calm and focused under pressure. During difficult situations, he remained a leader—in charge of his crew. Interestingly, the wire-pushing instrument called the "Billy Bob Pickle Fork," used in orthognathic cases was named after Dr. Hiatt. But I will remember him for the positive impact he had on my career as a surgical assistant.

The opportunities to be a part of many TMJ consultations and eventually to dictate the clinical notes became some of my proudest contributions. I wrote a letter to the medical director of a health insurance company asking for benefits for phase II treatments, for Paula, one of our TMJ patients, who had previously received denials for this coverage. This four-page dictation went into great detail, explaining the OMS surgeons' clinical findings, previous reversible treatments, recent magnetic resonance imaging (MRI) results, and the proposed surgical procedure. But most importantly, I recall being very candid as I explained that surgery is not a substitute for other treatments; rather, it is the treatment of last resort, either when other methods have failed or simply have not worked. I remember putting so much time and thought into this letter because I, once, also needed effective letters written on my behalf. I understood the need to get insurance coverage for TMJ procedures on a very personal level. I saw Paula's pain and I vividly remembered being in her shoes so many times myself. The end result of my letter was ultimately getting approved for surgical intervention. When I stood in the operating room helping with her procedure, my heart was content because I knew this covered procedure would offer Paula the best chance for significant pain improvement, function, and comfort. After twenty-five-plus years, this patient remains pain-free and still keeps in touch with me, her former surgical assistant. Just to think, our friendship started with an honest and open letter written to an insurance company, many years ago.

My surgeons invested in staff training, so they expected us, as a team, to successfully manage the unexpected. When I started my career in 1993, Brevital was the most common barbiturate used in most OMS offices and it had an increased tendency for laryngospasms. We trained for laryngospasms; we knew how to prevent them, but we also knew how to manage them, as a team, if they occurred. My surgeons modeled good judgement, remained focused, and demonstrated expertise at all times. This view taught me to appreciate the importance of staying in control during emergencies. These surgeons always stressed that we didn't train because we expected emergencies, we trained to prepare for emergencies. Our proficiencies are seen in routine procedures, those that we perform frequently, because familiarity breeds confidence. Our deficits are revealed when skills are not mastered. Failing to familiarize fosters an element of uncertainty. I know from experience that opportunities to handle office emergencies confidently come from frequent hands-on teaching and training.

Opportunities to develop my surgical skills continued but only because I was willing to jump in and learn, even after hours. I stayed late on many nights to help with emergency work-in patients. One particular case stands out in my mind. A man called our office to inquire about setting up an appointment for an extraction. After the receptionist scheduled him, he asked to talk with one of the surgical assistants. I was at the office, doing our evening follow-up calls, so I took his call. After asking key questions and listening to his symptoms—limited opening, high fever, severe pain, and swelling under his tongue and down his neck—I decided that this call needed to be discussed with my surgeon right away.

A gut instinct told me that this appointment could not wait a few days. We had this man come into our office without delay that evening. I brought him back into the procedure room and quickly recognized that this man presented with a widespread odontogenic infection extending from a lower posterior tooth. He appeared to be experiencing respiratory distress, so I called for the resident and surgeon to join me immediately in the room. Upon their prompt evaluation, it was apparent to them that this man presented with classic Ludwig's Angina.

That evening, I assisted them in the hospital operating room with tooth number thirty-one extraction and surgical drainage of the infection. The resident and the surgeon's quick thinking, surgical intervention, parenteral antibiotics, and airway protection all played a critical role in saving this man's life. The lessons that I learned were the importance of always listening to patients, asking key questions, and reaching out without hesitation, to the appropriate source, when concerns arise. It was an opportunity to see that employing good judgment affects patient outcomes.

The exposure assisting with trauma, orthognathic, and TMJ cases was a learning opportunity for me. I remember how before heading into the operating room to assist with my first open joint case, I nervously stood scrubbing at the sink with Dr. Ed Mosby. He noticed my apprehension and then he gently smiled at me and said, "I don't know why you are nervous, you're not the patient this time." Looking at me with piercing eyes, he passionately told me, "Learning is a lifelong process. Be patient, humble and teachable and you will be successful. Always be passionate about what you do and do it well." I miss his smile and sense of humor, but his advice and wisdom will always continue to influence my career. I can still hear him saying emphatically to me, "Go get 'em, tiger."

Working alongside the OMS residents also provided an environment of continual learning opportunities for me. We spent hours closing cases, trimming models, fabricating surgical splints, tracing cephalometric films, articulating models, reviewing charts, and preparing for surgeries. We unanimously recognized that each patient encounter was an opportunity to learn and contribute to exceptional patient care. We walked into surgeries side by side and we left together, having accomplished the cause we all supported, excellence in OMS.

Familiarizing myself with bone plating systems, navigating through dental implant systems, assisting with FCS procedures, and learning to take quality intra-operative photographs accurately in order to capture teaching moments, were all learning opportunities that helped me develop my hands-on skills. However, one of the most valuable opportunities came from watching surgeons interact with patients as they utilized their interpersonal skills. I saw these surgeons reach patients on a different level when they conveyed compassionate care, communicated effectively, listened attentively, and employed empathy. This view encouraged me to value and utilize these skills, too, because their impact was far-reaching when it came to patient responses and outcomes.

When I saw surgeons expect quality patient care from their staff, it reassured me that how patients were treated in their office took precedence over everything else. These surgeons placed value on leading a well-trained team and they knew this team would support a culture of excellence, if they led its members in the right direction. They also created an environment where I felt comfortable asking questions and supported my efforts by providing feedback on my performance. They climbed to the top, taking their team with them only because they employed good judgement and had an unwavering commitment to lead. These surgeons weren't without struggles, but they knew how to embrace uncertainty by recognizing their limitations and navigating together, through challenges, with the team they had so passionately developed.

Many surgeons also supported a culture of excellence through article contributions, authoring chapters for books, and speaking engagements at AAOMS national meetings. I remember reading their stories and listening to their presentations, which always left me with a sense of deep connection. Their messages were so intentional and riveting, especially when their views supported office-based anesthesia safety, to support the single-operator model as well as patient care and practice management issues. Some of these surgeons also encouraged me to write and speak and, because of their continual support, I joined them in their efforts to contribute to this specialty. Their motivation was contagious. These surgeons were role models, believers, and achievers. I also saw surgeons as teachers, educators, and mentors who were not only supportive to their surgical staff but to young residents in training, who would someday walk in their shoes. Their messages always echoed the need for steady hands, caring hearts, patient safety, strong business skills, staff appreciation, and inquisitive minds. That's what you needed to be successful; any missing link stood in the way of achieving this success.

The opportunities when I saw surgeons explain to patients that they were not ideal implant candidates showcased the surgeons' honesty. Turning away an opportunity to perform a procedure because it wasn't the best fit for the patient, or when better options were available, showed integrity. These surgeons were not driven by financial ends. Instead, decisions were made by recognizing how their patients' needs, would best be served.

I have listened to surgeons explain to their patients very candidly, why office-based sedation would not be a safe option. Putting safety first by employing good judgement is undeniably in the best interest of the patient. Patient selection criteria determined if a patient was a candidate for office-based anesthesia (OBA) and these assessments, performed by surgeons, were unquestionably, always held to the highest standards.

I have been in consultation and procedure rooms when more discussions were necessary to answer patient questions. Listening to surgeons address these concerns through further explanations supported better patient expectations. These conversations proved that open and honest communication builds trust. These surgeons did not want their patients to feel rushed, pushed, or confused when making treatment decisions. Instead, they wanted their patients to be comfortable moving forward and to be happy with their final results.

My exposure to FCS practices and their patients helped me better appreciate and understand the struggles of the aging face. I saw how extrinsic factors, such as years of sun exposure, as well as intrinsic factors, such as a decrease in skin elasticity and collagen breakdown, all influenced facial appearance. I also learned about standards and proportions and how creating facial harmony and balance supported aesthetics. I was fortunate to stand by surgeons who listened attentively to the unique needs of their cosmetic surgery patients. Sitting in on consultations and hearing patients articulate areas of concern made me more aware of how our perception of ourselves impacts how we feel. No doubt understanding this concept helped me become more sensitive to the needs of these patients. Listening to surgeons explain cosmetic procedures taught me the importance of effective communication and the critical role it plays in setting realistic expectations. Nothing builds a cosmetic practice better than a referral from a satisfied patient.

I also saw surgeons' commitments and passion never

waiver when cases were taxing and days were long. When tying one more suture, injecting one more site, pulling one more tooth, placing one more implant, making one more cut, bonding one more expose and bond bracket, writing on one more chart, placing one more call, and dictating one more letter seemed daunting, these surgeons remained focused on the task at hand. This view taught me that when you enjoy what you do, and the staff that stand by your side embrace your vision, nothing can hold you back. It's been an honor standing by surgeons who have invested so much of their time and talent to develop my career as a surgical assistant. I am forever grateful. Looking back, these golden career opportunities were priceless.

Chapter 7

Lead By Example

MANY OMS SURGEONS influenced my career as a surgical assistant, but one surgeon empowered me as a patient. This surgeon did not teach me how to hold a suction tip or retract for procedures because I never had the opportunity to assist him. However, the life lessons he taught me as his patient were more far-reaching and valuable than any of my opportunities or experiences as a surgical assistant. These lessons defined courage, supported perseverance, encouraged acceptance, and summarized compassionate patient care. They influenced my response as a patient and were influential in shaping my career. So how do you measure the positive impact someone has on your life? You simply can't. It's something you feel in your heart, something you hold onto and treasure, forever.

Recently, I had the opportunity to sit down and reconnect with my retired surgeon. It was not your typical meeting-of-the-minds discussion, as no attention was given to mid-line shift or chasing condylar hyperplasia. This conversation centered solely around my gratitude for the exceptional care he had given me, as his surgical patient, over the past thirty-one years. Without a doubt, our exchange of words was sincere and long overdue. I am confident that not many surgeons get the chance to sit before their patients, many years later, to hear words of appreciation.

I remember the silence that surrounded us, as we sat at his table with our chairs closely positioned. His attentive eyes met mine, as my voice cracked, mustering the words, "Thank you for everything you have done and for never giving up on me." Tears quickly filled our eyes. This shared moment was powerful and meaningful for both of us. The hand that once held reciprocating saws, screwdrivers, bone plates, and sutures, now reached across the table to hold my hand, as we recalled so many challenging surgical procedures. The only signs of our surgical history were seen in faded Risdon incisions and a midline shift: both visible reminders of difficult surgical procedures and unpredictable outcomes. I don't think he realized the impact he had on my life until we shared this moment, years later, hand-in-hand and heart-to heart. My words were intentionally delivered and I knew he sincerely appreciated hearing them because he told me so. We both needed this moment.

I always envisioned the day my surgeon would retire as being so far away; but in reality, this day had already passed. I wanted him to know how much he positively impacted my life. I met him when I was seventeen years old, a time when

I was mentally broken and physically exhausted from two years of failed surgical procedures. I came to him with my heart in pieces. I felt like a football that had been punted, passed, and kicked from surgeon to surgeon. I was in chronic pain and needed honest answers. But more than anything, I needed hope. This surgeon embodied that hope. He was dynamic, compassionate, and professional. I had built a wall high around my heart after so many previous unsuccessful surgeries, but this surgeon was able to connect with me. He saw my pain and heard my voice, but most importantly, he believed in me. His job was not only to navigate through a challenging surgical game plan but also to reestablish my confidence and trust in this surgical specialty. He quickly recognized the urgency to restore a young teenager's life, one that had been so disrupted by a rocky surgical history which started at the tender age of fifteen, with TMJ implants and osteotomies.

Little did I know that over the next few years, more surgeries would be necessary to get my train back on track. This surgeon stood by my side, leading his surgical team with unsurpassed skill and knowledge, as they performed long and difficult TMJ procedures, osteotomies, rib grafts, and ostectomies. The frequent letters, dictations, phone calls, and connections with me at annual meetings with other surgeons, to discuss treatment options, all meant so much to me. He even had me join him when he was administering oral reviews in Chicago, once again to re-evaluate, discuss, and formulate a treatment plan, after gathering feedback from other surgeons.

He simply never gave up on me. Once he jokingly said that he had more to do with raising me than my own parents during my later teenage years, because I spent so much time under his care recuperating from jaw surgeries. He also joked that he had more influence on my appearance than my own parents because of all the reconstructive procedures he performed.

His trip to Kansas City in May of 1996, to assist with my bilateral ostectomies, was the ultimate act of kindness. I will never forget watching him walk off the airplane carrying a green surgical towel that cradled his favorite osteotomy instruments. His willingness to perform a tough surgery away from his home operating room and staff and to help me recover afterwards were examples of his unwavering commitment to provide exceptional patient care. I witnessed the depths of his disappointments when my surgeries continued to have unpredictable results. The frustration and heartbreak in his eyes were apparent. Yet at the same time, he recognized when I needed moral support and he gave me the boost to forge on. He was always straightforward and honest with me and explained that the more procedures he performed, the lower the expectations. The risks involved were always made very clear. Many years ago, he supported my decision not to undergo any more jaw surgeries. Accepting life-long orthodontic retention with retainers, splint therapy, physical therapy, and composite veneers are all a small price to pay for comfort, function, and aesthetics.

I learned so many valuable life lessons from this surgeon over the years. Success is not measured in millimeters or mid-lines but rather in the quality of life one lives pain-free and functioning. Sometimes imperfect is perfect. Beauty is truly in the eye of the beholder. He taught me that disappointments should never define anyone but instead these experiences should be used to shape us and to make us all stronger and better. Together, we refused to accept failure; instead, we re-defined success. One of the greatest lessons he taught me was never to give up, to make the most of every situation by embracing and accepting outcomes, no matter the outcome. The words I heard so many times from this surgeon, "Take what you have and make what you want," will always hold a special meaning.

The little girl he empowered as a teenager is all grown up. I will always remember him as my surgeon because I will always be his patient. Time has not stood still for either of us. Today, over thirty-one years later, he is still standing by my side as a friend and mentor, coaching and encouraging me as a surgical assistant, to support a continual culture of excellence in OMS. My surgical journey is proof that not all challenging patients have poor outcomes. Some even become surgical assistants. When confidence and trust are restored, they change the scenery. I hold this specialty in the highest regard, and I will always be a voice of advocacy.

It is an honor to have this surgeon's continued influence and presence in my life. I am a better surgical assistant because of the surgical journey he walked with me. I modeled my career around his values: compassion, exceptional patient care, integrity, and dedication. He always set the bar high, and I am forever grateful for his unconditional support, surgical expertise, and wisdom. The positive impact he had on my life was immeasurable. His surgical skills were exceptional, but his interpersonal skills were outstanding. He demonstrated the true meaning of high-impact OMS; I saw it on a very personal level, from a patient's perspective. May we all learn to lead by following his compelling example. Dr. P. J. Walters—you are one of the greatest oral surgeons I will ever know.

Chapter 8

Exceptional Patient Care

WHEN WE DELIVER exceptional care, it has a positive impact on patient responses. I know this from my own experience as a patient. Technical skills are necessary to support quality care, but our interpersonal skills—those of listening, understanding, compassion and empathy—are often overlooked and forgotten. We must also never forget the value in empowering patients through education. Bringing together all of these skills are needed to provide outstanding patient care.

When we listen to patients, we understand their needs better. We learn a lot through listening when we take the time to be attentive and hear the patient's story. We do this by giving patients our undivided attention. Listening opens doors that may have never opened if we had not offered them the opportunity to be heard. Understanding patients facilitates diagnosis and treatment. It also builds rapport and offers assurance. Showing compassion is also important because it shows a sense of connection and conveys care and concern. Compassion also builds relationships and comforts patients. Providing this emotional support can improve patient coping skills. Expressing empathy helps us connect with patients by building confidence and trust. Patient satisfaction and compliance increase when staff are empathetic to their needs.

Showing patients simple acts of kindness can affect their acceptance of treatments and their response to them. When we pay attention to needs, we are better able to influence results. As a surgical assistant, I have had many opportunities to hold an apprehensive patient's hand and offer words of encouragement; both actions were necessary to get them through procedures. Remember, words are just as important as actions. Without a doubt, the OMS team can positively impact patient outcomes by delivering exceptional care through compassion, listening, understanding and empathy.

Empowerment through education also supports exceptional patient care. Providing careful explanations by utilizing effective communication helps patients better understand the message we are trying to convey. Maybe we are explaining post-operative implant care or discussing pre-operative prophylactic antibiotic instructions—whatever the discussion, we focus on empowering the patient to understand their care so that the best outcome is achieved. Educational opportunities empower patients. Continual guidance and consistent support by staff will encourage patients to take ownership of their treatment plans and recoveries. This personal involvement is critical because it connects patient understanding and participation to their treatment outcomes.

A powerful example of educating patients can also be seen in how well we deliver post-operative pain management instructions. While narcotics can be useful in managing pain, we don't want to dismiss the use of over-the-counter medications if they are a safe alternative for the patient. It is important to explain that nonsteroidal anti-inflammatory drugs (NSAIDS) and acetaminophen are preferably the first line of defense. Recent studies indicate that these medications are far more effective than narcotics in managing acute post-operative discomfort. It is the surgeon who determines the appropriate medications, but it is the surgical team who helps communicate that message to the patient.

It is critical to explain to patients that an opioid-free pain management goal is ideal. This mindset is necessary to aid in the fight against the opioid epidemic that currently rocks our nation. The role the OMS team plays in supporting this endeavor is to ensure that post-operative instructions are clearly communicated and understood. Equipping patients with knowledge supports better outcomes.

Exceptional patient care is not something we stumble upon by chance. It evolves through utilizing technical and interpersonal skills as well as empowering patients through education. Recognizing the importance and impact that these skills have on supporting optimal patient outcomes are critical to every OMS surgeon's success. Patients notice when the care they receive is exceptional and this should always be our main concern.

Chapter 9

He Nailed It

SOON AFTER I started my career, Dr. David Moore told me that the gold was found in the players, not in the practice. Years later, after seeing the positive role and impact that staff had on supporting a culture of excellence, I knew that he was right. Without a doubt, the greatest asset in an OMS practice is a well-led team and it is the surgeon who must lead this team.

You need staff who support your culture, embrace your vision, and follow your lead. They are the greatest influencer of your success. Put the best players on your team: those who want to learn because they hunger for knowledge and those who aren't afraid of stepping up because they welcome challenges and willingly accept responsibilities. A high-impact practice provides high-quality, patient-centered care. You need a committed team to help you carry out this task. Talented staff members are needed to provide exceptional patient care. Hire quality staff members, reward them fairly, and continually invest in them through teaching and training opportunities. Remember, salaries need to be aligned with experience, responsibilities and ongoing contributions. The value you place on staff is reflected in their compensation packages. Staff expect fair salaries and patients assume that competent staff assist with their care.

Staff training starts with a structured onboarding process. When it is rolled out, your onboarding plan should support not only the training but the maintaining of staff. Learning is a lifelong process and so is investing in staff training. Spend time developing your team, not dismissing one. Learn to build each other up, not tear each other down. Find the things that bring you together, not what separates you. Celebrate what connects a team and eliminate what divides a team. We are all stronger and better when we work together. The empowered team shares knowledge, communicates effectively, and values relationships.

Don't look for perfection; instead, look for improvement. Chasing perfection drives one crazy. Continual development drives success. Develop staff by teaching them to connect the dots by thinking wisely. The real value in staff members is apparent when they can identify the cause and effect in situations before they unfold. For example, we know ineffective suctioning can contribute to laryngospasms. Effective suctioning can prevent this airway emergency. Thinking ahead is the best prevention, but it also prepares us to handle situations, should they arise.

Keep your team sharp by encouraging continuing education opportunities. Learning ceases when we don't support or value education. Knowledge is best utilized when it is shared with the sole purpose of empowerment. Embracing change within your team stimulates practice growth. It encourages us to look at something from a different view; sometimes this shows us how to do something safer, better, and more efficiently. For most of us, embracing change is difficult, because it requires stepping out of our comfort zones; try it anyway.

Leading a team also means being able to connect with its members. Staff members need to see that they are contributing to something, and they require frequent feedback recognizing these contributions. The surgeon's reaction to their actions supports this connection. Staff also need to see that the bar is set high because the surgeon—the leader—expects excellence. A team will choke if leadership is not set in place because there is nothing to keep them grounded, focused, or connected. Being a good role model is important when you are leading a team. Constantly coach and encourage your team to give the best of themselves and make sure their view of you, the surgeon, is worthy of duplicating.

Nothing derails a team more quickly than allowing toxic behavior to occur. For instance, interactions that exhibit an unwillingness to help teach new staff or those who are always looking to watch a team member sink need immediate attention. These actions must be corrected, not tolerated. A high-impact practice does not align with toxicity. Early recognition and action are the key to extinguishing this situation. Learn to identify weak links and fix them right away because these situations, when overlooked, will lead to high staff turnover. They are costly and not productive to the practice.

The team that keeps your office running, even when you are not there, is the team that sees your vision, feels your passion, embraces your strengths, and supports your weaknesses. They are the first contact patients have with your practice and they can seamlessly coordinate scheduling, confirm appointments, verify insurance eligibility, and ensure collection of payments. They will come in early or stay late without hesitation and they will reach across the chair to hold a hand to offer comfort to a patient, without being asked. They set up trays, gown and glove you, confirm procedures, assist with airway management, suction, and pass instruments; they have your best interests at heart. This is how a high-impact OMS team operates. Never take them for granted. The role they play in providing exceptional patient care is priceless. The insight that Dr. Moore shared with me many years ago, about staff being the greatest asset to a practice, was accurate. He was spot-on and he nailed it.

Chapter 10

Standing By Your Side

A SKILLED SURGICAL ASSISTANT is one of the greatest assets in an OMS practice. Continual development of the surgical assistant to contribute to patient safety, quality of care and procedural efficiency is paramount to office success and supports risk management, which also protects the OMS anesthesia team model. A seasoned assistant values lifelong learning. There is no greater teacher than experience. Experience that is credited to time invested by the oral and maxillofacial surgeon to develop staff. The experienced assistant has been trained in how things are done, understands why things are done, and appreciates how applying these skills support patient care. The well-rounded surgical assistant can articulate clearly what services the profession provides, why the specialty is unique, and how this discipline distinguishes itself from all others. Success finds those who are knowledgeable, dedicated, and teachable. A competent assistant is vital to the success of oral surgeons; they can't do their job without us.

The surgical assistant must be proficient and competent in many skills in order to provide quality care. Proficiency in health history retrieval, systemic disease implications for upcoming surgical procedures, surgical assisting, patient monitoring, pharmacology application, and office emergencies are all critical skills and knowledge that must be mastered.

Competencies need to be visible at all levels, not just in technical skills but also in interpersonal skills. We must never forget the value and impact of these often overlooked and forgotten skills of listening, understanding, compassion, and empathy. Proficiencies with all of these skills have earned the surgical assistant an indispensable spot on the OMS team.

The assistant's precise eye-hand coordination is demonstrated during a tedious expose and bond procedure. The extra set of eyes to see a root tip proves helpful because sometimes the assistant has a better view, along with the steady hand that gently retracts and facilitates the removal of that retained root tip. When alerted that the inferior alveolar nerve is within reach, we cautiously withdraw the suction, knowing to get out and stay out. The assistant knows to irrigate copiously on the bur because overheating the bone is undesirable. Our keen instincts to reach for hemostatic agents and the electrocautery when hemostasis is challenged prove savvy. When the tooth to be extracted is in question, calling a time out to re-confirm the procedure reduces error and prevents wrong-tooth extraction cases. To facilitate efficient workflow, the confident assistant anticipates the next instrument and passes with smoothness and confidence. We continually and delicately follow suturing, as the tissues are seamlessly approximated.

The proficient assistant retracts so that the surgeon has a better view, suctions to maintain a dry field, and always protects the airway. We also realize that effective suctioning and placing throat pack partitions reduce the risk of laryngospasms and foreign body aspiration. Prevention supports risk management. Our trained ears differentiate crowing from wheezing sounds; regardless, our response is prompt. The attentive assistant motions with a nudge, a gentle reminder to the surgeon, to remove the throat pack after finishing a long case. Looking out for the patient and surgeon is habitual.

The role we play in gathering a thorough health history is critical. Well-versed assistants recognize the impact of systemic disease on office-based anesthesia. They also place value on accurate and timely charting because meticulous documentation will prove valuable in a possible deposition. We realize the importance of securing and maintaining an IV line. It is the most ideal and utilized path to administer medications and fluids. We understand the implications of losing this lifeline. The first drug in an emergency is oxygen, so we always check tanks. The assistant appreciates the value of an organized crash cart, especially in emergencies. We can identify, dilute, and draw up emergency drugs quickly and accurately, but always under direct supervision. To avoid misunderstandings, we utilize closed-loop communication by repeating the order, addressing questions immediately, and requesting a role change if the order is out of our scope. We know that benzodiazepines and opioids are reversible and we know that Flumazenil and Narcan are reversal agents. Familiarity with emergency drugs and equipment can be lifesaving. A sedation patient is never left unattended because we hold responsibility and accountability to the highest standards.

Our electrocardiogram (ECG) interpretation skills are precise, we can recognize critical cardiac dysrhythmias. Pediatric Advanced Life Support (PALS) reminds us that hypoxia is the most common cause of pediatric bradycardia. We know less cardiac functional reserve and resilience influences this phenomenon. Advanced Cardiovascular Life Support (ACLS) taught us that atrial fibrillation is the most common dysrhythmia in the geriatric population, so we question the use of antithrombotic drugs and are prepared for the possibility of brisk bleeding during surgery. Monitoring sedation courses have stressed that early crisis recognition is vital to effective airway management. Changes in patient status are detected through constant patient assessment. A knowledgeable assistant knows that pulse oximetry and capnography don't treat patients, they alert us to dangerous trends. We treat the patient, not the monitors.

We recognize the importance of maintaining the airway because if we don't have one, nothing else matters. We are aware that respiratory events almost always precede cardiac events. The key is never to lose an airway, because recovering one may be difficult. It is not the certificate on the wall that prepares us for emergencies, but frequent immersion in hands-on training and practice. The well-prepared assistant can apply office-based anesthesia knowledge and clinical skills in an emergency; both support the OMS anesthesia team model. In a crisis, we possess the calmness to think quickly and act appropriately. Unquestionably, we are trained and skilled to assist in stabilizing a patient, prior to 911 arriving.

Experience and intuition tell us when to reach out and hold a hand. Words of encouragement reassure uneasy patients by providing comfort. Our ability to implement quality care above and beyond procedures is invaluable. The ideal assistant exhibits leadership but never demands the spotlight. A humble presence can make a big impact. We are supportive and considerate of co-workers and convey respect and loyalty for the leader of the team, the surgeon. When we make mistakes, we own them and accept re-direction; both actions build character. When discussing concerns, questions, and expectations, we find the right time and place. Tough conversations earn respect when handled with professionalism. Effective communication supports everyone's growth. The experienced assistant shows good judgement during difficult cases. Instinct tells us to remain composed and focused. Sometimes saying nothing says everything. Silence prompts reflection and regrouping. When encouragement is needed, we offer a reassuring smile. Everyone needs positive affirmation. When asked questions about diagnosis, potential risks, and expected outcomes, we respond to the patient with a simple and honest answer: "Those are great questions for the surgeon." We know boundaries and recognize our skill set limitations. Deliberately and relentlessly, the surgical assistant supports a culture of excellence in OMS through procedure efficiency, impeccable safety, and exceptional patient care.

Developing high-impact surgical assistants through frequent training and teaching opportunities is a practice investment. A team that is sharp, connected, and committed will also be effective, safer, and better. The true value of a competent OMS surgical assistant is knowing that they are standing by your side and they have your back—this is priceless.

Chapter 11

It's Where My
Heart Beats

OFFICE-BASED ANESTHESIA IS one of the greatest services an OMS practice can offer to its patients. This privilege, earned through intensive training, is vital to the livelihood of this specialty. The ability to provide effective pain and anxiety management to patients is a need that has always existed but a need that must be met in a safe environment. Preservation and protection of the single-operator model should never be taken for granted. It must be held to the highest standards and delivered with safety, confidence, and effectiveness.

A comprehensive training program extends beyond just anesthesia training. It first starts with the surgeon's practice vision to build, lead, and engage the team—a plan for excellence that encourages the surgical team to weave purpose, commitment, and passion into every aspect of patient care. Leadership from the surgeon is a key component to attracting and retaining top-quality staff that will engage in training and support the anesthesia team model. Surgeons who expect excellence will get excellence. The ability to lead a team is critical in developing a team.

Facilitating the development of competent surgical anesthesia assistants through teaching and training opportunities remains imperative. A well-led and trained surgical team brings significant value to office-based anesthesia safety. It is crucial that the surgical team deliver high-quality, office-based ambulatory anesthesia. The surgeons must have a highly trained team to accomplish this goal, which requires continual leadership, preparation, and simulation.

Development of the surgical anesthesia assistant begins with the surgeon. Staff will respond to a surgeon who clearly communicates the expectations and provides support and who shares his or her knowledge. Teachable and trainable moments elevate the practice. Constant immersion in training is the single most important element to emergency preparation and management. Skills are mastered with confidence through in-depth knowledge, understanding, and frequent performance. Training for excellence prepares staff for the unexpected. Skills are improved through constant review. This review gives an assessment of our proficiencies and deficits. Identifying the gap between what we have mastered and what we need to master is critical. Part of the training plan needs to fill that gap.

So how is training for excellence in office-based anesthesia achieved? By teaching, practicing, and demonstrating skills used in anesthesia administration. Frequently providing the surgical team with opportunities to expand knowledge through hands-on training and evaluation is an effective way to measure and master skills. Recognition and management of office emergencies are both essential to successful outcomes. Recognizing and responding to emergency situations are fundamental skills that must be mastered. In an emergency situation, everyone must be comfortable in performing their role. Training as a team ensures that each staff member understands their role and how to interact with other staff to achieve the desired outcome. Team training also builds relationships, trust, proficiency, and confidence.

There are many resources today for training and developing the surgical anesthesia team for excellence. DAANCE, developed by AAOMS is a core educational curriculum geared towards training the surgical anesthesia assistant for office-based anesthesia and sedation assisting. The Anesthesia Assistants Review Course (AARC), sponsored by AAOMS, is a comprehensive live, in-person review course that emphasizes essential anesthesia protocols and guidelines. A condensed version is also available online. AARC also prepares the surgical assistant for the DAANCE examination. The Anesthesia Assistants Skills Lab (AASL) for AAOMS allied staff provides hands-on training with anesthesia administration, airway management, dysrhythmia recognition and medical emergency management.

AAOMS also offers its members an in-person course on Advanced Protocols for Medical Emergencies that discusses emergencies encountered in the OMS office setting and the participation of the assistant in these situations. Finally, the Basic Emergency Airway Management (BEAM) simulation program offers real life emergency airway training for the OMS office-based sedation team. The state-of-the-art technology integrated into this program evaluates performance and provides feedback on skills. This training simulation program offers cutting-edge resources to train the OMS team on the delivery of safe office-based anesthesia.

State approved monitoring of sedation courses for the surgical team are also a great resource that support effective office-based anesthesia training. ACLS and PALS certification provide a systemic approach to advanced resuscitation efforts through recognition and evaluation of algorithms, airway management, and pharmacology administration. Local, state and, national dental meetings and webinars provide opportunities for continuing education and hands-on labs skills for anesthesia administration and crisis management. All of these resources are valuable in supporting positive patient outcomes.

Continued development of the surgical anesthesia assistant to be cognizant of basic sciences; anatomy and physiology; patient evaluation; medical concerns encompassing cardiac, metabolic, nervous, immune, and pulmonary systems; drug administration; crash cart organization; emergency drills; sedation levels; airway management; equipment monitoring;

algorithm recognition; and emergency treatment protocols all warrant attention. Understanding and mastering these core competencies through practice and review should be strongly supported and encouraged by the surgeon.

Training for excellence is a balancing act that takes time, commitment, and dedication. Every OMS practice that administers office-based anesthesia needs a team that is proficient in rendering this service. Recognizing where the surgeon needs to take their team to foster this culture of excellence is mission critical. The defining moment for a team should never be a "wake-up call" in an emergency situation that they are not prepared for, but rather in an emergency situation that is handled with calmness, expertise, and professionalism.

The message that every surgeon needs to hear from their surgical anesthesia staff is apparent: "We are united as an OMS team, affirmed with leadership under your guidance and driven to reach the highest standards to deliver exceptional patient care. We stand by your side as a unified surgical team. We are prepared for the unexpected, we are confident, and we are well-trained in the delivery of office-based sedation. Stay calm doctor, we've got this."

Comprehensive training and maintaining superlative safety records will distinguish our efforts to promote, advance, and protect the office-based anesthesia team model. The path taken today to validate training of the surgical anesthesia assistant will positively impact and influence the direction of office-based anesthesia privileges. Raising the bar by implementing and supporting anesthesia training standards and protocols for your office will lead the way for successful management of office emergencies. We all need to commit to the continual development of the surgical team to model excellence in office-based sedation through teaching and training opportunities. Emergency preparedness and management are paramount to supporting a culture of excellence. It takes all of our efforts to preserve the privilege of delivering office-based anesthesia to patients. I know it's where my heart beats.

Chapter 12

These Are The Things That Matter

D URING THE DAY-TO-DAY hustle and bustle of running a practice, it's easy to lose sight of key focal points. We all need to remember that our success is dependent upon how well we embrace the things that matter. Building a high-impact practice from residency through retirement requires a continual process of adjustments and adaptations, learned through perseverance and earned through an unceasing commitment to provide exceptional patient care. Success is first determined by adopting the right attitudes. Attitudes not only encourage how we view and support processes but also how well we implement and maintain them. The culture you adopt defines your vision, displays your passion, supports your beliefs, and leads your team. Culture is the greatest influencer of success. No amount of marketing strategy can make up for a lack of vision or culture.

Sometimes we think that having state-of-art facilities is critical to this success. They aren't. It's not the surgical suites or the latest technology integrated into your office that build a high-impact practice. Instead, it is the practice culture and the staff that stand by your side that have the most influence on success. Patients may not understand the value of a cone beam computed tomography (CBCT) scan or the benefits of platelet-rich plasma (PRP) machines, but they do understand how you made them feel before, during and after a procedure. That feeling has little connection to square footage or technology. What a patient sees and feels inside practice walls is what matters. Show them teamwork and synergy, not chaos and confusion. Let them feel compassion and comfort—nothing less.

Leading a team is never without challenges; it's not an easy job. Leadership is not about being the best; rather it is the desire to lead and make everyone better. Captivate and connect with your team by providing feedback and always cultivate a hunger for knowledge. Spend time developing staff because strong relationships are the building blocks for any practice. Successful people find the right fit for themselves, but they also carve a spot for others because they see the value in working together.

Take the time to develop your staff members and to get to know them. If you feel like something is getting out of control, it probably is and it needs immediate attention. Gut instincts are usually right. A lack of team dynamics will quickly derail a team. Time spent attempting to recover staff that can't be resuscitated is poor time management, because finding a rhythm when there is no beat is a futile task. Nothing will drive a great employee out the door more quickly than watching an employer tolerate toxic behaviors.

You need a dedicated and talented team to stand by your side so that you can provide quality services. Your surgical skills have no value if you can't deliver patient care. You can't do this job alone. A team is only effective if roles and responsibilities are clearly defined, understood, and carried out. You can't teach experience; experience comes from opportunities. The skills needed to perform surgeries are different than the skills needed to lead a team. We strive to perfect our technical skills, but we need to also work at perfecting our interpersonal skills. These often-overlooked soft skills are the ones that matter the most.

Perfect situations can go wrong. We need to be prepared to handle the unexpected. Training makes the unplanned situation easier to handle. Things will happen that are out of our control; however, our responses to these situations are in our control. It's not the certificate on the wall or the card in your pocket that prepares you for office-based anesthesia emergencies. It's the frequent immersion in training that prepares us to handle the unexpected.

Always remember that there is certainty in change, and we need to be open to accepting this change. When change is initiated, expect temporary chaos, and be prepared to navigate through uncertainties. Routine is our comfort zone. Change is our uncomfortable zone. Both zones are necessary for growth. The struggles lie in failing to implement change because it's easier always to do, what we've always done.

Acquiring and carrying too much financial debt can weigh you down emotionally. It can also be paralyzing to the practice. Make wise decisions that support healthy financial strategies. When decisions are based solely on satisfying productivity targets instead of meeting patient needs, you are driven by the wrong reasons. Remember, productivity is not as important as responsibility; and in the end, we are all responsible for providing exceptional patient care. These services must be in the best interest of the patient. We all hunger for patient volume but may we always thirst for exceptional patient care. It is this quality care that will build your practice, one patient at a time.

Stand out among competitors by being compassionate and patient-focused, not because you have the biggest or newest facility. Don't worry about being the busiest practice in town; focus on offering high-quality services. Success is not only about getting patients through your doors; more importantly, it's how well you treat them, once they're inside. Always maintain high standards in patient safety and surgical expertise. Remember, it's okay to not know all the answers. Rapport is established through honesty and integrity. Every struggle, every doubt, teaches us humility; some of the greatest lessons evolve from these experiences. Modeling humility by embracing a humble presence reveals more about a practice's culture than any procedure performed. Practicing humility opens the doors for referrals. Never forget the importance of establishing, building, and maintaining your referral base. Let nothing impede this opportunity.

Don't spend too much time capturing the perfect moment to post on social media. Instead, spend time creating the best patient experience, in your office. That's the most credible platform. Tweets and other social media postings lose their effect over time, but exceptional patient care leaves lasting impressions. We make great effort pushing practices into the social media spotlight. May we always remember to put that much energy into delivering compassionate patient care. Never underestimate the power that lies within your practice doors. The most powerful marketing tool you will ever have already stands by your side.

Surround yourself with staff members who can help create balance and encourage office harmony. We all perform better when we support each other. No matter what day to day pressures we all face, it's our relationships with people that ground us. In every successful practice, there will be good days and bad days. They are both important because one teaches appreciation and the other teaches perseverance. When you feel like you are running on empty, take a time out to re-charge and re-frame. Hitting the re-set button is always an option.

When the direction you are headed in, no longer serves you, be comfortable pausing and re-framing. This is accomplished by being in touch with yourself. Awareness of how you feel and what you are thinking is closely connected to your performance. Acknowledging mental health should never be shunned; it should be front and center. Remember, before you can take care of your patients, you first need to take care of yourself.

Balancing your professional and personal life is critical to your success. Your career is not your sole identity; it is only a part of who you are. Life will always pull you in different directions. The pressures both at the office and away, will constantly demand your time and attention. These challenges will always be present, but they are manageable. Work hard, stay engaged, seek adventure, find a hobby, and always remain humble.

Do we all dream too big? Probably not. Do we want too much, too soon? Probably so. Find a balance and a flow that work for you and stick with them. The only way to get better is to keep moving forward. The choices we make are reflected in the chances we take. We learn by observing and we respond by doing. High-impact practices are influenced by a vision that supports a continual culture of excellence. These practices don't settle for less; they accept and embrace more. Please remember, these are the things that matter.

Chapter 13

Thinking a Different Way

THERE ARE REASONS why some OMS practices succeed
and why some struggle. High-impact practices set themselves apart from others. But how do they do this and why
does it work?

A practice's success is first rooted in establishing an office
culture. It is a vision that clearly defines core values, beliefs,
and attitudes. Articulating and supporting this fundamental
mindset is the foundation for success. Exceptional patient
care should always be our main concern and invariably the
end result of the services we provide. We all must be committed to this cause as we head out of the gate.

Setting yourself up for success is something that evolves
through careful planning, calculated decision-making, and
putting the right processes together and executing them.
Identifying a practice vision, establishing a business plan,
building a talented team, providing leadership, and finding

passion in your work are all critical components. High-impact practices set realistic goals that are attainable, trackable, and measurable. Recognizing that the road to success is never easy, they manage challenges and expect detours. They constantly pay attention to the direction of their practice. Noticing what takes them forward and identifying what sets them back are equally critical courses to track.

High-impact practices attract, develop, and retain quality staff members. They know the value of putting the best players on their team and because of this, staff turnover is rare. The onboarding process for employees supports the office culture and integrates the practice vision. Expectations and roles are clearly defined and understood. Effective communication is also visible and continually encouraged. Improvements need discussion and accomplishments need recognition. High-impact practices play to win by bringing their team members to the top, together.

They know that their greatest asset is the team that stands by their side every day and they never take this for granted. Continual investing in their team—the heart and soul of their practice—needs no convincing. It is visible who influences their success. Empowered teams serve patients well and in return these satisfied patients build practices.

High-impact practices have specific team attributes that influence their positive outcomes. Understanding the importance of applying them is critical to achieving success. When looking at a successful practice, there are distinguishable and palpable team characteristics that stand out such as enthusiasm, competency, motivation, trust, and adaptability. The members of a dynamic team will perform at a higher level because they recognize and communicate feelings that evoke healthy emotions. In return, a good team builds positive relationships with co-workers, patients, and the referring community. Remember, the most influential marketing team already works in your office.

High-impact teams are coached by the practice leader. They teach and develop critical skills and provide feedback by using effective communication that creates an environment where staff feel comfortable asking questions. They constantly infuse their team with knowledge, support, and affirmation because they appreciate and understand the intimate connection between coaching a team and achieving success. This inspired team will help lead a practice to greatness. Coaching skills are far-reaching, powerful and practice-changing, if staff allow themselves to be led and coached by those who are willing to invest in them first.

High-impact teams understand the importance of meeting and nurturing basic human needs. Consistency, whether in procedures or expectations, supports an environment of certainty. Challenges stimulate growth and self-fulfillment. A sense of importance promotes self-worth and encourages confidence. Connection brings a team together and supports cohesiveness. A happy and balanced team achieves greatness by recognizing these needs. They place value in building, strengthening, and maintaining strong relationships that are crucial to office harmony and positively affect patient care.

High-impact leaders think differently; they approach success from a different view. They don't aim for the grand prize as they head out of the gate; instead, their main focus is placed on developing each other. For example, before building a high-volume implant practice, the first investment is placed on building and developing the team. It is that dynamic team who will get the practice to where they want it to go as an implant industry leader because they appreciate processes, understand expectations, communicate effectively, and value relationships that are vital to growing a successful implant business. That's how we hit the jackpot and build high-impact practices.

High-impact leaders demand honesty and respect from their team. They set an example by treating their staff with dignity and integrity. Interpersonal relationships are intricately intertwined with both team and patient interactions. How we treat co-workers is mirrored in our delivery of patient care. Positive staff interactions breed and support quality services. Practicing emotional intelligence by employing good judgment, respecting boundaries, and recognizing limitations benefits everyone.

High-impact teams can perform under pressure because they have been trained on how to approach challenging situations. Struggling teams sink under pressure and their performance crumbles because they have not been coached on how to handle uncertainty. When properly trained people are at the helm, they stay afloat in troubled waters because they have the skills and confidence to navigate any situation successfully. Empowerment through coaching will always prove valuable. There is no greater investment than the commitment to develop staff members who will help lead your team. A confident team is comfortable performing roles, remains focused under pressure, and can accept re-direction. Its members support, respect, trust, and motivate each other.

High-impact practices understand that every patient deserves exceptional care. They recognize that quality services are not influenced by referral base or patient status. Instead, equal treatment for *all* patients is embedded into their core practice values. The commitment to serve these patients is not a job description; it is their culture.

High-impact practices understand that it is the patient that hires them. They realize that building a practice occurs one patient at a time. Every patient encounter is an opportunity to market the practice internally. These offices understand that everything they say and do matters.

High-impact practices are driven by a vision. These practices bring their team to the top without ever looking back. Failure is never feared because it is not an option. Mistakes are viewed as learning opportunities, not setbacks. Uncertainty is not a concern, but rather a catalyst for clarity. Risk is an opportunity, not an insecurity. Competition is not a threat, but a challenge to keep pushing ahead. Change is embraced to encourage continual development. These practices don't stop, they pivot and adjust, to get to where they need to go.

High-impact practices are not immune to rising costs and declining reimbursements. They utilize savvy business strategies and execution measures to offset and manage these constant financial challenges. They remember that keeping one step ahead is better than being one step behind.

High-impact practices recognize that as a provider, their landscape will always be changing. The hurdles of running a practice are high and so are the expectations. Competition will not go away; it is fiercely here to stay. Competitors are no longer just other OMS surgeons. Instead, it is an open range. Increased regulatory compliancy continues to add more pressures and paperwork to the already-existing, intimidating workloads. Escalating costs and shrinking reimbursements are daunting. Doing more with less in return is a harsh reality. Offering affordability, maintaining cost effectiveness, and delivering efficient services must remain an integral part of the equation. Most importantly, patient safety must always earn a stellar rating. Leading a team successfully through continual change is a critical skill that pulls a practice forward.

High-impact practices understand the challenges of running a practice. They know some of these challenges are inevitable. Schedules fall apart because cancellations happen. Patients are no-shows and treatment plans change. Busy times are cyclical and referrals sometimes sluggish. Procedures may take longer than anticipated and the waiting room fills up. Staff shortages occur when people get sick or employees depart. Equipment malfunctions and autoclaves overfill. Supplies are on back-order when they are needed the most. Pandemics are never planned in advance. Computers crash and cybersecurity attacks happen. OSHA comes knocking and HIPAA constantly demands. Software upgrades are necessary and often costly. Guidelines change and protocols are rewritten. Technology constantly evolves—in with the new, out with the old. Implants sometimes fail and root tips are occasionally retained. Dry sockets happen and expose, and bond brackets fall off. Most patients are pleased, but some will never be satisfied. Not all consultations turn into procedures. You book some, you lose some. Some things cannot be controlled, while others must be mastered.

High-impact OMS practices succeed because they understand that combining the right attitudes, ideas, and processes aligns with success. They support a continual culture of excellence by thinking differently. Successful practices embrace, nurture, and develop their practice and team as they continue to evolve into something dynamic and unstoppable. Thinking a different way changes the outcome.

Chapter 14

This Story Could Be
Anyone's Story

SOMETIMES THE HARDEST stories to share are often the most important ones to hear. The handwritten letter that I received from one of my OMS friends became a chapter in this book. The letter summarized this surgeon's history with substance abuse. He believed sharing his story was important; after reading his letter, I knew he was right. His experiences were poignant and at the same time comforting because by sharing his story, he offered hope. We all need to point towards hope.

I've known this surgeon for many years. Our friendship has stood the test of time. He saw the depth of my passion to help build high-impact practices when I leaned on him for manuscript advice, review, and support. I saw his steadfast commitment to this specialty, when he willingly shared his personal struggles with addiction, with the sole purpose of helping other surgeons. We both knew we could tackle writing this difficult chapter together, because we both passionately supported a culture of excellence in OMS.

This chapter is raw. It is real and it is necessary. There is a message here for everyone: a message not buried, but instead, painfully obvious. The best way to tell someone's story is by stepping into their story, with them. I was honored to listen to this surgeon recount his personal struggles with addiction but even more honored to stand by his side as a friend and share his story in this book.

He began to abuse alcohol and narcotics during his third year in the OMS residency training program. Residency was stressful. At times, patients were really difficult to manage. Working long hours contributed to sleep deprivation. Meeting tight deadlines and managing heavy workloads were not easy tasks to juggle. Anxiety levels at times were high and the day-to-day pressures were often overwhelming. He frequently self-medicated with narcotics and alcohol to alleviate stress and relieve depression. Although his intentions started out rather innocently, these behaviors quickly led to addiction. He hid his addiction, telling others that he suffered from headaches and depression. This excuse was his convenient cover-up, but it was far from the truth. Reaching out for help was challenging because he felt that resources were not easily accessible. The fear of getting kicked out of the OMS residency training program was always front and center, and so were having severe restrictions placed om him. Looking back, years later, he realized that it is a much better decision to self-report your addiction. The consequences are less severe, and you usually can avoid media coverage and widespread public disgrace. One month before completing his residency, he sought treatment, on his own, for depression and headache management. That's the story he told his program director, but he was really seeking treatment for addiction. Eventually, after completing his residency, he did share his addiction struggles with his program director, who was very supportive.

He learned to hide his illness because he did not want his colleagues to view him as a failure. Very few, if any, knew about his addiction because he kept it well hidden. However, some may have suspected he struggled with addiction because his behavior patterns occasionally signaled concern. However, none of his colleagues intervened, most likely because he was so convincing that he was okay. He was a respected resident, well-liked and kind to his patients. Everybody loved him. He even received the Resident of the Year Award, but he felt guilty accepting this award because he had just completed a thirty-day, in-house addiction treatment program. Feelings of unworthiness flooded his head, because silently, he was an addict.

Upon discharge from that treatment facility, he immediately began using alcohol and narcotics again. Addiction is like a magnet, powerful and pulling. Young, talented, and educated, he accepted a position with a private-practice OMS office to begin what he hoped would be a long and successful career. Sometimes what we hope for isn't necessarily what we get. He didn't think his OMS partners suspected that he had an addiction problem, and nothing was mentioned. Again, he hid the elephant in the room well. His abuse of alcohol and narcotics continued to spiral out of control.

About a year later, he checked himself into a six-week, two-to-three nights a week outpatient rehabilitation facility. He wanted to get better. He reached for hope. He found respite from his addiction illness for three years. During that time, he was enrolled in the state's Physician Health Program (PHP), which required weekly and sometimes twice a week urine drug screens (UDS). He was also required to attend twelve-step recovery meetings, both Narcotics Anonymous (NA) and Alcoholics Anonymous (AA). He was grateful for the support that these organizations provided him. He doesn't think that he would have discovered NA or AA on his own. These support groups became his lifeline. Today, he is still a supporter of NA and AA; when he attends these meetings, it is not because he has to, but because he wants to. Support also came from counselors, family, friends, and colleagues. No battle should ever be fought alone. He was also required to meet with the PHP for monthly meetings and a counselor more frequently. His life improved tremendously, as did his relationships with those around him, with these support systems set in place.

But after three years, the PHP monitoring agreement ended, and he quickly slipped back into relapse—proof that diligent monitoring plays a big role in achieving and maintaining sobriety. Without a doubt, there is measurable value in long-term monitoring, and it is a necessary service, not only for the physician's health but for patient safety. Today, many PHP agreements have been extended to five years or more due to the high rate of relapse when monitoring ceases at the third year.

When monitoring ended, he relapsed, hard. His colleagues were now well aware of his substance abuse struggles. Desperate to turn his life around, he took a leave of absence from this busy practice and checked himself into a three-month inpatient addiction center. Checking into rehabilitation facilities over and over again, became recurrent events. Each time, he felt broken, hopeless, ashamed, and fearful; but he was never alone, ever. On several occasions, there were also other oral surgeons seeking addiction treatment with him. In fact, one of them was his roommate during a long-term rehabilitation stay. They have remained close, lifelong friends.

After completing three months of treatment, he felt optimistic and confident about his future. After all, he was drug-free and both physically and mentally stronger. However, his return to private practice was not easy. Many referring dentists stopped sending him patients. His tumultuous addiction history was now known by many in the dental community. The stigma of being an addict stood out. Instead, it should have been his hard work and personal growth during recovery that attracted attention; but they didn't. He was doubted by many and, at times, he doubted himself; but others stood by him and supported his return to work. It was that support system that gently lifted him up. Nobody wanted recovery more than he did and nobody deserved it more.

However, upon returning back to his private practice office, he relapsed again. This time, his addiction had spiraled out of control. Blackouts robbed his memory. There were days when he was unable to recall events. A near-death experience while driving his car to a satellite office to see patients was a wakeup call. In the blink of an eye, he missed hitting a cement barricade under a bridge head-on. He almost died but it wasn't his time. The rippling and devastating effects of addiction rocked his personal and professional life. He was fired from his job. His relationship with his wife was strained. The deception needed to cover up his addiction ultimately destroyed his marriage. His wife divorced him. Addiction is a serious illness with high price tags. The implications are far-reaching. In a short period of time, this surgeon lost his wife and job to addiction—but he did not lose hope.

He consulted with PHP again. They were his only hope and they immediately suggested long-term treatment. After completing six more weeks of in-patient therapy, his counselor referred him to a half-way house to continue to live in a recovery environment. He worked in a furniture store for two years, earning minimum wage. Then a substance abuse counselor position opened up and he took that job. After spending three years in a halfway house, he was able to rent an apartment from his sponsor. He continued to attend meetings every day and fellowshipped with people who were also recovering from addiction. His entire time in long-term recovery was spent working hard at recovering. He knew this was his most important job. Reflecting on the poor choices he had made and taking accountability for his actions played a critical role in his recovery process.

His comeback was in waiting. The journey to get to where he wanted to go was not easy. It had never been easy. His road to recovery was long and hard but he never stopped believing that the best was yet to come. This surgeon never lost hope to someday practice OMS again. He always kept his continuing education current and remained board-certified. There was something flickering deep within his soul—even in his darkest hours. A spark was all he needed to light his path and show him the way. He had this trait: it is called tenacity. He felt strong and was ready to start his career.

So, he applied for his dental license. He was denied. This was no doubt disappointing, but not career-ending. He then applied in another state for his dental license. He was completely open and honest with the board. He was given a consent agreement with several monitoring requirements. These included weekly UDS for three years with decreased frequency over time. He was also required to attend counseling sessions and NA and AA meetings. A pharmacist would need to come to his office every day, to inventory drugs.

He was so grateful for the opportunity to practice OMS again. Now, he just needed to find an office. He had a lead from a friend on a potential practice to purchase, which happened to be hundreds of miles away. Timing was every-thing. It only took one phone call to set things in motion. It was the new beginning he had longed for. He packed up and moved his few belongings. Getting started would not be easy. Financial struggles greeted him, but he did what he needed to do, to make this opportunity work. There were sacrifices. He slept on an inflatable air mattress, alongside a pellet stove, to keep himself warm. Suddenly, things gradually started to fall into place. He applied for his DEA license and started making plans to open his office. His malpractice insurance increased by 50 percent because of his addiction history. But every year it went down by 10 percent. He hired staff who were compassionate about delivering exceptional patient care and taught them about addiction and what to look for, should he relapse. All of the staff were required to read his consent agreement. He set the bar high and put the best players on his team.

Six months later, he opened his doors and saw patients for the first time in six years. During the first few weeks he felt apprehensive, but each day got better and better. He soon realized that for the first time in his career, he could honestly say that he loved practicing OMS. It was a new start, a humble new beginning for this surgeon. He led his team with purpose and passion and practiced successfully for almost thirteen years. He said these were his best years of practicing OMS: proof that it is possible to reach the pinnacle of your career after experiencing recovery from addiction. Recently, he was forced to retire due to other health reasons.

He struggled with not only substance abuse issues but also five different cancers throughout his career. He was diagnosed with Hodgkin's Lymphoma shortly after completing residency. About fifteen years later, he was diagnosed with

B-cell Lymphoma. Five years after that diagnosis, he had kidney cancer. Three years later, aggressive bladder cancer and prostate cancer were diagnosed. Treatment for these cancers involved a combination of radiation, chemotherapy, and surgical intervention. He applied the same principles that he relied on in addiction recovery to get him through these health challenges. Acknowledgment, accountability, hope, and a dependable support network are powerful tools. A strong spiritual program is also paramount to any recovery process. These guiding principles can be applied to any challenges in life. He tried to come back after his most recent cancer diagnosis and treatments, but he recognized that taking care of himself was his most important job. Life has not been easy for him. I've never once heard him complain. His attitude and perseverance have been remarkable.

The letter he shared with me and the follow-up phone calls will forever be embedded in my heart. There are no words to adequately describe how honored I am to have connected with this surgeon and to be his friend. He built a bridge of hope by openly sharing his story of addiction. One voice can impact many.

Remember, we are all pilgrims on a journey. We are
travelers on the road. We are here to help each other
walk the mile and bear the load.
—"SERVANT SONG"

His final message is something we all need to hear. Addiction can happen to anyone. It does not discriminate.

It is a disease process not a weakness or a lack of willpower. If you are abusing alcohol or drugs, reach out and talk to someone and seek treatment. Don't delay. Do not let the fear of shame prevent you from reaching out for help. Addiction is a lifelong illness. Recovery is a lifelong process, but neither are lifelong impairments.

Although his OMS career was not as long as most surgeons, his contribution to this specialty is far reaching. This surgeon gave us something no textbook could teach—transparency and hope through personal experiences. He braved the wilderness for all of us. Remember, this story could be anyone's story.

Check online resources for Alcoholics Anonymous (AA) and Narcotics Anonymous (NA) meetings. Consult the websites: https://www.aa.org/ and https://na.org/ for information on local chapters. Your state Physician Health Program (PHP) can also be a good resource.

Chapter 15

Crossing the Finish Line

EVERY SURGEON HAS a career story. It's been a privilege for me, to be a part of many of these stories. The memories of building practices, leading teams, and providing patient care are connections to their past. They never abandon you. Many surgeons can recall their first procedures and most their last. Many remember difficult cases and others try to forget. Some recall patients who have challenged their surgical skills and some remain lifelong friends. Many watched their practices evolve from humble beginnings and many became industry leaders. Many weren't afraid to take chances because they knew that they built their practice on a solid foundation and that support system would stand the test of time. Many embraced changes because they were confident that the end results would be favorable. Some expected too much, too soon and they quickly learned humility. Some changed the direction of their practices and they eventually soared. Some were content walking away, while others still yearned to perform one more procedure. The significance is not in starting or finishing, it's everything you accomplish along the way. That's how you define yourself.

We must never forget those who have crossed the finish line without ever receiving any accolades for their continued support and dedication to this specialty. Sometimes it's the contributions that go unnoticed, that make a significant impact on an organization. Maybe you wrote an article, presented a speech, trained a resident, developed a surgical assistant, or empowered a patient. Maybe you shared your struggles to help build a bridge of hope for other surgeons. Whatever your contribution was, it mattered. We rise together because no task is accomplished alone but through the collaboration of minds all seeking the same cause—high-impact OMS. The opportunity to soar comes from watching and interacting with people who have led us to better places. Never forget that the greatest contribution is your legacy, one that can inspire a new generation of surgeons to contribute to a continual culture of excellence.

In the end, it is the people you affected and the relationships you built that matter the most. When the familiar sound of the drill is no longer heard, when the grip on the forceps is no longer felt, and when your keen eyes are no longer needed to retrieve a retained root tip—may this day greet you with the same enthusiasm as your first day, many years ago. Remember, it is the beginning of your career that connects you to the end and everything in between is your story. May crossing the finish line be an affirmation of a job well done. Together, we all can answer the call to build high-impact OMS practices.

Acknowledgments

THE OPPORTUNITY TO soar comes from watching and interacting with people who model excellence. I learned from top-notch surgeons who invested countless hours teaching and training me. I connected with the most beautiful souls and I am a better surgical assistant because of their influence. I am grateful to those who have invested their time and talent to help me develop as an oral and maxillofacial surgical assistant.

To my first employer, Dr. David L. Moore: you were the first oral surgeon to see the spark in my eye and the hunger for knowledge that gripped my soul as we stood side by side, procedure after procedure. Thank you for sharing your expertise and talent and developing me as a surgical assistant. Looking back, these golden opportunities were career-defining moments.

To Dr. Ed Mosby and Dr. Bob Hiatt who have gone before us, too soon: I am grateful and honored for the opportunity to have stood by your side as a surgical assistant during many TMJ and orthognathic procedures. Your skilled hands and wisdom influenced and developed many residents as well as my own surgical assisting skills. I think of you both often. Rest in peace, my friends.

To Dr. Ed Laga: thank you for your continued friendship and encouragement to write this book. Your exemplary courage and strength are an inspiration to many.

To Dr. Mark Flack: you were a big part of my career and I will never forget your positive influence. When I came to you with questions or to seek advice, your door was always open. Thank you for sharing your wisdom and for encouraging me to never give up on my passion to help build high-impact practices. I will be watching you cross the finish line from a distance, but rest assured, my heart will be right there with you. Stay close, my friend.

To Dr. Adam Flack: your honesty, integrity, and commitment to provide exceptional patient care are remarkable. Thank you for setting the bar high for all of us.

To the OMS surgeons, surgical teams, and business staff members with whom I have worked throughout my career: thank you for your friendship and countless learning opportunities. Together, we saw the value of teamwork and its positive impact on providing exceptional patient care.

To Patty Francy: you were one of my biggest supporters in writing this book. Thanks for reminding me that my message is important and needs to be heard.

To the OMS offices who welcomed me into their practices over the last several years to observe and discuss practice management and to those who connected with me at national meetings: thank you for your transparency and willingness to share your practice struggles and success stories with me. Your contributions to this book are invaluable. We can't do this alone.

To my Dental Assistant Program instructors at Northeast Iowa Community College, Gloria Kluesner and Tina Adams: thank you for teaching me the foundations of dental assisting. You set the bar high in the classroom and expected excellence in clinical applications. That knowledge and those skills remain embedded today, in my career.

To my publisher, Henry DeVries and the team at Indie Books International: thank you for walking me through the publishing process. Your expertise and guidance made this book possible.

To Mark LeBlanc: thank you for the many coaching sessions over the past few years. Our conversations taught me that listening is one of our greatest skills.

About The Author

MARTHA DUNLEVY PETERS brings a unique perspective in defining a culture of excellence in Oral and Maxillofacial Surgery. Her experiences come from both sides of the dental chair. She understands on a very personal level that the services we provide must be exceptional. Spending most of her teenage years as an orthognathic and TMJ surgery patient, influenced her decision to become a surgical assistant and fueled her passion to help build high-impact OMS practices. She has twenty-seven years of oral and maxillofacial surgery assisting experience which includes clinical, hospital, and surgery center settings. Martha is passionate about developing the surgical team to model excellence in all aspects of patient care. Martha has trained and developed many surgical teams with the goal of always achieving safety, efficacy, and confidence, which support positive patient outcomes. She has a special interest in office-based anesthesia training and team development through coaching and has published articles on these topics.

Martha is a graduate of Northeast Iowa Community College. She is a member of the American Dental Assistants Association, Missouri Dental Assistants Association, Missouri Dental Association (associate team member), Greater Kansas City Dental Society (team member), and American Association of Oral and Maxillofacial Surgeons (allied staff member and clinical interest group member). Martha is DAANCE, ACLS, PALS, BLS, Missouri Sedation Monitoring and Missouri and Kansas Nitrous Oxide Monitoring certified.

She is a native of Northeastern Iowa, having grown up near the banks of the Mississippi River. Currently she resides in Kansas City, Missouri with her husband and five children. She can be reached at mdunlevypeters@gmail.com or (816) 516-0777.